The Third Opinion

Stephanie,
Choose to thrive,

For Stephanie —
Blessings to you!

The Third Opinion

A Story of Faith and Family

J. Stephen Mikita

Published by
Wings Publishers
3555 Knollwood Drive
Atlanta, Georgia 30305

Text ©2000 by J. Stephen Mikita

All rights reserved. No part of this publication may be reproduced, stored in a retrieval system, or transmitted in any form or by any means—electronic, mechanical, photocopy, recording, or any other—except for brief quotations in printed reviews, without the prior permission of the publisher.

Book design by Robin Sherman
Cover design by Nicola Simmonds

Manufactured in the United States of America

10 9 8 7 6 5 4 3 2 1
First Edition

ISBN 0-9668884-9-9

Foreword

If life is just a series of lessons learned, Steve Mikita is the last stop sage on top of the mountain. What could really be more important than unbridled enthusiasm for life? How could anything propel us happier toward the finish line than zapping the absolute most from every millisecond we live? How much better most of our lives would be if gratitude for what we have replaced uncomfortable yearn for what we do not. Steve not only has those gifts, he knows where they came from.

The best things in my life are the people who have passed through it. My magical children and husband, of course. Family and lifelong friends. Many others . . . some through routine daily activity, others met because of exposure afforded me by my job.

It's been an interesting and often unforgettable menu of personalities. Some who have accomplished great things in arenas completely foreign to me. Others carried with them an envious and reassuring air of spirituality. Still another group was simply physically beautiful. I've been blessed with the cross section and took something from each, but from none no more than I have received from Steve Mikita.

It takes only moments, perhaps a sentence or two, for a complete stranger to forget Steve Mikita's physical difference and be caught up in the rest of him. Instantly, you feel that he knows you. Not just what you put out there for show and tell, but you sense he knows who's dancing backstage. Does such a gift come from adversity itself or does it spring from shepherds intent on beating back the demons of defeat with a club of worth? I don't know, but one thing could not be more clear; gratitude, hope, and joy for life are personified in the author of this book.

Adages become so primarily because they ring true. Make the most of what you have, enjoy every minute and on and on. We have these homilies stuck on the refrigerator and embroidered on pillows. Easy to read, just as easy to send down the hall to the waiting room when the frantic of life intrudes. Not so easy to dismiss when the best of adage is a man.

The Third Opinion is a real life medical thriller set against the backdrop of a classic and extraordinary American family. An incredible journey, an incredible man. This book will change you because you will want it to.

Leeza Gibbons

Introduction

From a very early age, I dreamed about writing this book. I just never thought it would be this soon. I told Mom during long, anguishing hospitalizations that I wanted to live long enough and achieve enough to be able to write the story of my life. I thought my autobiography would be written during my retirement years, when I was 60 or 70. I believed it would symbolize my final hurrah, following a long life of accomplishment and success.

Some of that plan has changed. My muscles are not that accommodating. At 39, it has become increasingly difficult for me to write, and impossible for long periods. I know it won't be long before I lose my ability to write altogether and I will be required to speak into a voice-activated computer. I suppose I could have waited until I had mastered this new technology, but that would have taken at least a couple more years. I am not confident that I have that luxury either.

I am getting weaker generally and I don't know how many years I have left. I am sitting on an anatomical time bomb that could go off any day. Consequently, while I still have the energy and the strength I am compelled to share the barriers overcome and the joys experienced in my life. Therefore, this book comes to you sooner than later.

I have never walked, never run, never danced and never knelt to pray. And yet, despite my weakening musculature, this is not a story about getting weaker and fearing death. It is about getting stronger. It is about choosing to thrive and not just survive. It is about reaching our possibilities, regardless of our disabilities. It is a story about courage and vision, it is a story about faith and family.

Chapter 1

During her pregnancy, Mom experienced no warning signs. Nothing irregular. After all, she had given birth to two previous children, Carole and Billy. Both of them were healthy and happy, as was the rest of my parents' life in the mid-1950s. Dad was a young, aggressive orthopedic surgeon in the tough, blue-collar town of Steubenville, Ohio, which was famous for producing steel, Dean Martin and Jimmy "the Greek" Snyder.

Mom and Dad's future seemed boundless, no impediments on their horizon, not even slightly. All of their familial and professional equations were balanced and simple.

My birth, initially, did nothing to disrupt, but only amplified the seamless comfort of their lives. I was a pre-Christmas bundle of normalcy, arriving only twelve days earlier than the predicted due date of December 26, 1955. But for this minor variance my entrance into life was unremarkable.

The delivering physician unequivocally proclaimed me "perfect" — an absolutely fit infant. There was no evidence to doubt the accuracy of his opinion. No reason to worry. No cause for concern, just a young, prosperous family celebrating another symbol of their good fortune.

For the first several months, I satisfied all the necessary criteria for babyhood. By all accounts, I was "good," "chubby," "strong," "responsive," "alert" and, above all else, "irresistibly cute."

In addition to these parental plaudits, I received impressive marks for my jovial disposition and athletic prowess. On cue, I began crawling like most of my peers. Expected, uninhibited development.

The Third Opinion

Natural, instinctual.

Suddenly, the alarm of adversity was subtly yet unmistakably triggered. In a single, innocuous act terror trespassed upon my parents' tranquility. I was eight months old when Dad reflexively reached under my arms to pull me off the floor. Unlike normally developing infants, my arms did not offer a firm, resistant grip. Instead, they floated horrifyingly upward above my head. I fell to the floor and the bottom fell out of our happy home.

In his practice, Dad had examined and diagnosed other childhood diseases. He feared that I had a type of muscle disorder because I was manifesting the symptoms of "floppy baby" syndrome. Rather than prematurely disclose his preliminary findings with Mom, he elected to observe me a while longer. He chose to hope against hope.

But as weeks passed neither he nor I could conceal the mounting evidence that something, everything was terribly wrong. It was obvious. I was different and my condition was not improving. Notwithstanding Mom's cheers and prayers, I demonstrated no inclination to stand, let alone walk. The moisture on my head was not the signal of my trying, but was from Mommy's crying.

Mom and Dad coaxed, coached and cajoled me. But my puzzling body was content to sit on the floor.

Next came the maddening and conflicting diagnoses. At fifteen months I was examined by a neurologist in Pittsburgh, who blamed my temporary inability to walk to a well-disguised maternal instability. Taking my father aside, he said, "Dr. Mikita, your son does not need a neurologist. Your wife needs a psychiatrist. This child is merely a slow-walker. If she simply backs off and quits pressuring him, John Stephen will walk any day."

So confident was he of this assessment that he admonished my parents not to cut my platinum-blond hair until I stood erect and traveled my first steps. Wildly desperate, both Dad and Mom overlooked his tactlessness as well as his recklessness regarding Mom's mental health. They agreed to follow his advice while they anxiously awaited my physical development.

They waited three months. They dutifully followed this first opinion. No pressure. No prodding. No bribery. They waited and yearned and prayed for that promised event. Each day would dawn with renewed hope that their nightmare would end. But there I sat, oblivious to both their turmoil and my uncooperative muscles.

Nothing was working. Their laissez faire strategy was utterly ineffective. I continued to defy all of their hopes and dreams. It was becoming clear. My inability to walk was not a question of would not, but could not. There was not a lack of desire, only a lack of strength. Psychology was not the solution. Chemistry and genetics were. Mom and Dad sought a second opinion. Dad painfully made two appointments. The first was with a battalion of specialists at the National Institutes of Health in Bethesda, Maryland. The second was with his barber. My hair needed to be cut. This decision was no ordinary childhood ritual. It was a solemn ceremony of surrender. It was a major act towards accepting that I was not a normal child. Whether or not I was walking, some aspects of life, such as haircuts, could not and should not be delayed.

At eighteen months I was a medical enigma who had survived his first haircut as well as the pricking and probing of an N.I.H. jury of physicians. Their verdict was as unanimous as it was devastating. They claimed I had a rapid, degenerative, neuromuscular disorder known as Werdnig-Hoffman Disease. It was incurable. It was terminal. It would kill me at the age of two. I only had six months to live!

Only three months earlier the Pittsburgh neurologist had reassured my parents that my body was on a brief, insignificant detour. He promised them that I would eventually find my way back onto the thoroughfare of health and development. Now they were being told that I was speeding uncontrollably downhill towards a sudden death. There was nothing either the doctors or my parents could do.

As they described it, first my voluntary muscles would be affected. Movement in my limbs would shortly vanish. Sitting up, even lifting my head, would swiftly follow. Finally, my involuntary muscles would fall prey to the merciless enemy. Utterly wasted and totally decimated, one night I would quietly pass away in my sleep.

The doctors were hapless. My parents were helpless. And my future? It was aimed directly, irreversibly toward hopeless. How unfair! How senseless! How cruel! How final!

Chapter 2

Helpless and hopeless my parents left Bethesda with this second opinion and began preparing for two future events — the birth of their fourth child and the funeral of their third. On that day, Dad cried long and hard. He felt totally powerless to reverse the inevitable tide of events that would kill me.

Although he was both gifted and wealthy, there was absolutely nothing that he could do but confront the painful reality that I was going to die. My supply of muscles was quickly being depleted. There was nowhere he could purchase new ones. Thus, tears were Dad's only option.

Mom and Dad began confronting the awful truth that their youngest son would never walk or run. I was not going to survive my second birthday. I was different and dying.

Mom and Dad met tragedy that day when the doctors issued their findings and conclusions in Maryland. But it did not leave them there. It accompanied them to Ohio. It ushered them into their house, up the stairs and even invaded the sanctity of their bedroom. And there it stayed. It lingered and hovered.

Then, the darkness began to recede. In the ensuing months following the startling news that I was dying, Mom and Dad grew accustomed to living with adversity. For the most part, life resumed its normal pace. After all, Dad's patients needed his expertise and time. My sister, Carole, and brother, Billy, required Mom's.

Death loomed over me, but I was distracted by an environment where love and optimism abounded. I don't recall anything the slightest bit frustrating or depressing about that time following our return from the N.I.H. I remember being kissed a lot, chinning myself with my elbows atop a revolving coffee table to attempt walking around it and dancing polkas every Sunday in the arms of my Uncle John. Most of all, I remember playing with my brother, Billy. With him as the perfect playmate, I never considered my imperfect body.

While awaiting my death, Mom and Dad decided to make the most of the time we had remaining. Their tears dried and what they saw was a child who was neither sad nor in pain. To their great relief, I was not worsening at the accelerated pace predicted by the physicians. I was not getting stronger. But I was not degenerating, either. My general health was excellent and my energy level was impressive. It was becoming increasingly apparent that I had been granted a stay of execution, no matter how brief.

I was healthy, happy and quite alive!

Chapter 3

What explained this sudden reversal? Had a miracle occurred? Had the doctors misdiagnosed me? It was bewildering and mysterious. But also exciting and thrilling. Was death just around the corner? Would the torment and torture return and end my remission? What accounted for this reprieve? Would my life be spared? It certainly was a miracle! Not a cure. I was not standing or walking. Even so, a miracle happened.

The fact remained that yesterday I was alive and the next day I might still be smiling and breathing. That was more than sufficient to qualify under the definition of "miracle." Admittedly, there were no heavenly visitors, lightening bolts, or revised medical forecasts. No magical medications. No scientific breakthroughs. No radical new treatments or exotic potions. But there was a life-changing event.

There would be a third opinion.

Dad chose not seek advice from another medical colleague. He had spent enough time in doctors' offices and hospital examining rooms. My future remained bleak, but it was worth one final investment. Dad spent his last quarter of hope on a magazine.

The inspiration for a third opinion was not contained within an obscure medical journal. It was discovered within a simple magazine. Just an ordinary magazine. The January 1960 issue of *Look* provided me with an extraordinary resource of hope and power and tenacity. It featured photograph after photograph of Franklin Delano Roosevelt, an American president in a wheelchair. It was a celebration of his legacy and greatness as a leader, warrior and inspirational giant.

Before I learned to say my ABC's, I learned to ask for FDR!

Beginning at the age of four, and every morning for two years thereafter, I faithfully took my morning dose of inspiration and motivation from my miracle magazine. I would wake up and ask Mom, "Give me FDR!" Although I had trouble enunciating the hard 'r', Mom knew what I wanted and needed.

There was no one else with whom I could identify and relate to in children's books. All of those characters were able-bodied and could stand, walk and run. Consequently, they were fantasies. FDR was about an exciting reality and, for me, an extraordinary possibility.

The magazine contained twenty-three pages of photographs of FDR, both the public figure and private polio victim. The front cover of the magazine showed his famous, confident smile that held the omnipresent cigarette holder. His head was tilted back, which evoked an aura of vigor and reassurance. Looking at these pictures filled me with more energy and adrenaline than any medication could.

Equally important was the empowering commentary that permeated this daily ritual. Mom and Dad not only helped me turn the pages. They also enumerated FDR's accomplishments and achievements. They used words such as "popular," "powerful," "influential," "strong," "leader," "father," "husband," "beloved," "great," "courage," "famous" in describing him. But the one I remember most was "fighter."

Listening to what he had achieved from his wheelchair made my own future something to look forward to, not dread. Also, I felt a keen sense of belonging. I felt special, not different; unique, not abnormal; excited, not afraid. I felt valued and needed.

FDR ascended to great heights. Mom and Dad issued their invitation for me to join him in making a difference throughout the world. I felt an overwhelming desire to live and have my life mean something. I couldn't wait for tomorrow to come, to learn more about FDR and listen to Mom and Dad describe how he triumphed in spite of his disability.

FDR was my map to manhood and my guide to greatness. He stirred my soul and chiseled my choices.

One day, Dad closed the magazine before I had completed my visual calisthenics. It was time to add another ingredient to the third opinion.

He said, "Stevie, you will never be able to walk and run like other children because you have extremely weak muscles. But you have a strong mind. You will never play football or baseball or basketball. But you can compete in the classroom and excel there.

"You must never feel sorry for yourself. You have been given a lot. You are better off than your two immigrant grandfathers, John and Stephen. John was born in Czechoslovakia; Stephen was born in Yugoslavia. They came to America when they were teenagers. They never saw their parents again. They had no money, no education, no knowledge of the English language. John earned a dollar a day working in the steel mill. Steve bootlegged whiskey during the Prohibition. There are less fortunate people than you." Then he concluded, "Don't be afraid, son. If FDR did it, then so can you."

It took less than two minutes. I was his congregation. It was one of the greatest sermons ever given.

In his characteristically succinct manner, Dad defined my life and directed my destiny. He told me who I was and what I could become. He described my strengths and pointed out my weaknesses. I learned that my mind could be developed even if my muscles could not. He said I was good at thinking and reasoning. I was not good at walking and running.

At four years old, I was given my balance sheet for life. I saw my assets and knew my liabilities.

However, of all the lessons taught on that occasion was the realization that I wasn't the only person who had to deal with adversity. Life had not unfairly picked on me.

Yes, I had a disability and obvious physical limitations. But I had other strengths, talents and skills. Dad told me I was no different than anyone else. I learned what challenges had confronted not only FDR, but also my grandfathers — my namesakes, John Mikita and Stephen Lazich.

They, too, had had obstacles and handicaps. They had language and economic and cultural barriers to overcome. They didn't have their parents' support nor someone to cheer them on like I did.

By comparison, my life didn't appear so overwhelming, tragic or sad. I could see I had advantages that my grandfathers didn't have. Mom and Dad would be there to help me and support me throughout my life. By giving me that magazine, they gave me an exciting example to use as a pattern for my life.

My grandfathers, despite all their roadblocks, had persevered. They didn't give up. They achieved their versions of the American dream. They succeeded, notwithstanding their disabilities. Their roads were not easy. Mine would not be hazard-free. There would be bumps and accidents along the way. After all, I would never walk.

But I had a choice. It was my challenge. It was my decision. It was my test. It was my life. I needed to take responsibility for my life. I needed to decide whether I was going to be happy or whether I was going to spend the rest of my life feeling sorry for myself because I couldn't walk.

No matter what the doctors had said or what Mom and Dad had told me about FDR, I was entitled to my opinion as to what kind of life I would live.

This was my opinion. The third opinion.

I knew if I concentrated on my strengths — what I could do — then I would succeed. If I pitied myself because of my weak muscles, then I would never see beyond my wheelchair.

Dad said they were all "fighters." No matter what, none of them ever shrank from the challenge. They were brave.

With them as my examples, my choice was clear. I wanted to be like FDR. He had not allowed polio to defeat him; I couldn't allow my weak muscles to destroy me.

Beginning that day when Dad had linked me to FDR and my pioneering grandfathers, I started planning for and looking forward to the future.

Dad focused my attention on the possible, that which I was capable of achieving in my wheelchair. He was also telling me to let go of the impossible, those things that I couldn't do because of my disability.

I dared to dream. I wanted to achieve. I chose to fight.

I didn't know it, but I had just taken my first steps.

Chapter 4

Although the third opinion provided a rough outline of what my life could be, there was a dilemma — FDR was an adult and I was only a little boy. His world was so far away from mine. Could I ever get where he was?

I didn't wait long and I didn't travel very far. At four years old, I found myself in my new baby sister's crib. I was given the responsibility of holding Judy's orange juice bottle. A high honor, indeed.

Each morning. Mom would lift me into that safe world of softness and smells where I would perform my duty. Judy was the first person who needed me, the first person I served, not to mention, the first person who I knew could do less than I could.

I was making a difference in someone's life. I was great at holding her bottle until it was empty. I understood the best angles that would reduce the risk of Judy getting too much or too little juice. My only thoughts were of her, for her, with her. I didn't want to make her cry because I knew that I didn't like to cry. I also had more time than Mom and Dad. They were too busy to hold the baby's bottle.

This was a job that I could do and wanted to do. I felt so important. I needed to get out of bed every day, not only because Mom wanted me to, but also because I had a job to do and felt that I did it better than anyone.

Judy and I were both nurtured from that bottle. It gave her certain nutrients and vitamins. It gave me my first taste of success.

In fact, I learned that my disability was not a hindrance. Access into her crib was provided by Mom.

Once there, there were no physical requirements I couldn't meet. Holding a bottle requires more emotional than physical skills. I wanted to get out of bed each morning to serve.

This opportunity thus allowed me to draw upon my strengths. Judy was very happy to see me. Mom complimented me for my performance of this very significant job. I was too concerned about Judy to worry about myself. That was Mom and Dad's job, along with that famous doctor we were going to visit in New York City.

With my fifth birthday fast approaching, it was time for another evaluation. Mom said, "We're going on a train to New York City tonight. You'll be staying up later than you ever have before! Let's get you in your pajamas and go to the train station."

When we got to New York the next morning, a taxi drove us to see Dr. Howard Rusk, the father of rehabilitation medicine. On the medical side, he could not issue a glowing report.

Rusk suspected that I had a neuromuscular disease, but he couldn't identify it. Yes, he agreed that I would never stand or walk. Yes, there was a likelihood that I would survive my fifth year. but he wasn't sure.

Although my particular disease wasn't diagnosed until a decade later, the explanation for it is quite simple. My muscles receive weak messages from motor nerves which transmit impulses from the spinal cord out to a particular muscle group. Because of these defective nerves, the muscles hear only "whispers," rather than the "screams" which are normally heard throughout a person's body. Consequently, my muscles cannot develop and instead grow weaker or "atrophy" over time from the lack of strong stimulation. In short, my muscles are lulled to sleep and not energized by my body's timid whispers.

Ironically, my sensory nerves are perfect. I have full feeling throughout my body. Even though I appear to be a quadriplegic, I am not paralyzed and have normal bodily functions. Because of my deficient motor neuron cells, I have gotten weaker each year. Seldom is that weakening visible to anyone but me.

It's frustrating to want your body to perform one way and know that it can't. So fear, failure and frustration are integral parts of my disease.

I believe that is why the discussion between my parents and Dr. Rusk shifted from medical speculation to fatherly advice. Dad said it was the best advice he and Mom ever received.

The Third Opinion

"Treat this child in the same way as you do your other three children," Dr. Rusk admonished. "Do not shelter or protect him from life's experiences. Allow him to play on the floor with his older brother. Even let his brother wrestle with him. If Stevie gets hurt or cries don't pick him up immediately. Let him work it out. Treat him no differently from his brother and two sisters."

Mom and Dad listened and learned.

When a child has a disability, the natural response is to center one's entire world around him or her. His or her needs become paramount. The parents' needs and other children's are forgotten or postponed. Dr. Rusk acknowledged that this was a common reaction, but bad medicine for everyone, especially the child with a disability.

His message was clear and unambiguous. Do not forget your needs and those of your other children. Maintain a healthy balance between fostering the disabled child's growth and satisfying his special needs. Yet, be careful not to devote inordinate amounts of time and effort towards him, to the exclusion of his siblings, so as to avoid making him too dependent, too demanding, too self-centered, too spoiled.

Early on I realized that I was very important to Mom and Dad. But certainly not their only priority. I was only one of four children. Not their only child, not even their only special child. We were all special in their eyes. I needed to share not only my toys with my siblings but my parents. I was not the center of the universe.

There was no hiding the fact that I was limited by my physical disability. Because I could not run or walk there were certain aspects of life that I would miss or not be able to perform with the relative ease of an able-bodied child. That was something I needed to confront. Mom and Dad were available to assist me in understanding these issues. But, as Dr. Rusk had explained, they should not insulate me from learning who I was in relationship to the world.

I was living in a physically-conscious world. That world, unfortunately, was not always hospitable to little boys in wheelchairs. Soon I would be off to school. There would be stairs, playgrounds and other children. Curious, inquisitive, tactless children.

Mom said, "Some kids are going to be afraid of you, not because you're mean, but because of your wheelchair. They probably have never seen someone in a wheelchair before.

"Other children will think that just because you're in a wheelchair that you can't think or talk like they can. Remember, when we've gone to stores and restaurants together and people speak louder and slower to you, they think you are mentally retarded. That's why I tell them to speak to you, not me. You're smarter than they think you are."

Even the most hurtful question or awkward one, such as, "Why can't you walk?" or "Did you break your leg?" deserved a response. Mom suggested, "Just tell them you have weak muscles, so you can't walk like they do."

Mom and Dad were extremely supportive, but they could not live my life for me. They were not physically disabled. I was. Consequently, I needed to take an active role, a leading role in the decisions affecting me. It was time to register for kindergarten.

Chapter 5

There were six kindergartens in our town. The first five rejected me. The teachers did not want me as one of their students. Too many unknowns, too much responsibility, too afraid. I wasn't welcome.

Mom and Dad remembered a veritable spark plug of a woman, Vi Walton, who had been Carole's kindergarten teacher.

Vi wasn't much taller than her pupils. But in that 4'8" frame was a tower of electricity and love. Mrs. Walton didn't hesitate; she couldn't wait! Of course, she would accept me.

But the School Board balked. Vi Walton's elementary school fell outside the boundaries of our neighborhood. Our home was on the outskirts of town and McKinley Elementary was at least five miles away. Vi telephoned my parents. She was sorry. Her hands were tied. She was distraught. Dad was outraged!

Dad telephoned the School Board and demanded that he be included on the next agenda. When he got his turn, several Board members voiced their concern that I would be attending a school in another district. After all, there was a policy that proscribed the transfer of any student to another district, they explained. Dad listened incredulously. He then stated: "This boy deserves an education and I will sue the hell out of this Board if you prevent him from getting one!"

The Board voted in favor of granting an exception to its general policy. The vote was not unanimous. Dad never forgot that night and never forgave the dissenters. He always said, "A good education is something worth fighting for."

J. Stephen Mikita

McKinley Elementary had plenty of stairs. But in 1961, architectural accessibility, especially in grade schools, was a distant dream. So, Dad would carry me in his arms each morning up the stairways and place me into a seat, next to my first girlfriend, Anita Lynn Kaufmann. "Nity" was flirtatious, cute and absolutely oblivious to my physical limitations. Even if she did notice, I never noticed.

Because of the stairs, I was a captive of the classroom during the two recesses. But Mrs. Walton made sure I wasn't left alone. She assigned two caring cousins, Danny Carter and Mike Sarap, to entertain me while the other children were outside.

Danny was quite a legend. He was the only five year old who looked down at the teacher. At 4'10" he towered over Mrs. Walton, and became a giant of a friend to me. Danny's cousin, Mike, was equally devoted. But they were not the only ones. There was Sid Carte and Bobby Leist. Each boy competed for my attention and sought my friendship. Sid was roly-poly. Bobby was a mischievous five year old.

Bobby also had a disability — hemophilia. I remember him missing a lot of school. I was sad that his hands and arms were always bruised from the transfusions of blood that he required. Mom explained that Bobby needed to be extremely careful not to injure himself. He had to safeguard against cuts and bruises because his blood did not clot as effectively as others. I knew that Bobby must feel frustrated at times, especially when he had to go to the hospital or convalesce at home.

I was glad that I just had weak muscles. I was happy being me! There was not much that I missed. I made friends easily and could keep them. I learned quickly how to find common ground and forge common interests. The other kids liked me as much as I liked them. My recesses inside seemed to be more than adequate, with the special feature of no teacher supervising me.

Naturally, at times I was unable to participate at all. Going down the sliding board (which was located inside the classroom), climbing onto the playground's merry-go-round (do not get the wrong idea; no music or horses — just a circular wooden plank with steel handles on certain sections from which children would hold onto in order to push the other children riding or standing atop the merry-go-round around and around) and attending school assemblies held in the basement gymnasium were not accessible to me.

The Third Opinion

Admittedly, at such times my throat would tighten, my heart would ache and swallowing became difficult. I wanted to be included. But those feelings and frustrations would soon pass. Replacing them were happier, more positive feelings whenever I would realize that I could do other things and being different had both its pluses and minuses. I could not have the good without tolerating the bad.

Without a doubt, the worst and most exasperating experience of kindergarten did not stem from my disability but from my inability to control my rambunctious, three-year-old sister, Judy, who was my first and only choice for show-and-tell day. She was an adorable, uncontrollable terror.

Disaster struck almost immediately after Dad departed. Instead of sitting next to her proud, immobile older brother, Judy began a rampage of pulling chairs out from under unsuspecting student victims. She did so with brute force and menacing delight. No matter how much I pleaded for her to cease and desist, she ignored me. Even Mrs. Walton's disapproving words and battery of admonishments were futile in the face of this toddling juggernaut.

Following my return home, I reported Judy's reckless disregard for human life and unequivocally stated to both parents that never again would I place myself under such embarrassing circumstances without the help of an army. Dad responded with a paternal pat-on-the-back as if to say you will not be spared exposure from any of life's pleasures, including an undisciplined little sister.

But my successes and failures were not just confined to the classroom or within the friendly confines of my home. My playground, a specially designed and modified one, was also fertile ground for my growth. Its architect was my brother, Billy. Only thirteen months older than I, Billy not only defined the rules of all my games, but also gave me my name.

Before Billy began speaking, I was referred to universally as John Stephen. Such a name was much too long and imposed myriad difficulties for a six-year-old brother to enunciate every time that he desired to engage me. He called me, "TeeVee" and the name "Stevie" stuck.

Baseball and softball equipment were much too heavy and cumbersome. But these were minor inconveniences to the commissioner of my game, who was able to adapt our love for baseball to the harsh realities of my muscle weakness. Billy discovered a game called "whiffle ball" that replaced wood with plastic and became a vehicle for our love of competition and mutual adoration.

The fact that I could not run was irrelevant. Our tomboy sister, Judy, would be assigned to be my legs whenever it was my turn to swing the bat. Since most of the balls I hit were on the ground, not in the air, then certain rules applied which enabled me to compete on an equal footing with the other able-bodied players from our neighborhood. It is significant, however, to note that I was afforded no unfair advantage over any of the players simply because I was sitting, not standing. I struck out, grounded out, flew out and, at times, was thrown out of games just like anyone else. I wanted to be treated the same, not differently, and was.

When it came time to take the field, there was only one position for me to play: pitcher. During my elementary school years, I was able to lift my right arm above my head with the help of my left hand and then throw my weight forward to propel the ball towards home plate.

I was positioned a little closer than the opposing pitcher, but that was a risk of the game I was willing to accept. Not infrequently, a ball would be batted into my face at a high velocity just after I had thrown it. But the stinging would soon pass after I struck out another batter!

When there were no other boys to play with, Billy and I would go out to our driveway and he would transform it into either Pittsburgh's Forbes Field, Chicago's Wrigley Field, New York's Yankee Stadium or San Francisco's Candlestick Park. Billy was not only the commissioner, but the greatest play-by-play announcer the game has ever had. Move over Harry Cary and Bob Prince (the legendary Pittsburgh Pirate broadcaster).

Billy was amazing. Not only was he blessed with a creative mind to alter the rules of the game in an equitable manner, he also had boundless energy to chase after his batted balls and mine. How we treasured those nights at our ballpark when the names Clemente, Stargell, Mantle, Maris, Mazeroski, Mays, Aaron, Banks and Williams would resound off our imaginary field.

To enhance the entire experience we would assume the batting stances of each of our heroes and adopt their every idiosyncrasy — minus the tobacco, of course! Bubble gum sufficed.

We played under the lights even when we had no lights. Billy was there to supply them, too. The lights, the crowds, the excitement, the electricity. Because of him, I knew the sights and the sounds and the boys of summer.

When the temperatures chilled and the World Series ended, the ballpark became a football field. Neither touch football nor tackle football was beyond my limitations or Billy's modifications. Whenever we played touch football, I was a receiver on offense and a designated rusher on defense. Have you ever tried to block a motorized wheelchair?

Since one hand was firmly placed on my joystick, I was permitted to touch with my free left hand while the others had to touch with two. Some people eluded me, but more times than not, the quarterback could not avoid my all-out blitzes. I took pride in playing excellent defense, long before the Steel Curtain made an art form of it.

The more interesting adaptations were made on the tackle football field. Because our front yard was sloped and (much to Mom's chagrin) not well manicured, my driving on it was too treacherous. That was a minor inconvenience for which Billy quickly compensated. We would both don our pads and helmets with Mom as my equipment manager and Judy assigned to take my place on defense as the rusher. She had already gained my confidence as my substitute not only from her speedy displays on the baseball diamond, but from that day of fire and fury in kindergarten. On offense, while Judy was catching her breath, I would be securely ensconced in my team's end zone at either end of our yard/field. I believe I have been on the receiving end of some of the hardest, prettiest spirals ever to drill through the air.

On one occasion, in order to catch a low pass, I dived out of my wheelchair, to my amazement and Mom's astonishment! It was not only a spectacular catch, but evidence of how much I wanted to compete.

None of these sports was for the faint of heart. Each game was marked by its intensity, woofing, trash-talking, heated rivalries and sibling sparring. One day we had just concluded a major football game prior to dinner. As we sat down, Dad commented that Judy appeared as if she had been tackling Jeff Spahn, who was already an outstanding athlete and went on to quarterback the high school football team and later play in college. Billy and I could hardly contain ourselves with the knowledge that that was exactly what Judy had been doing quite successfully all day. We were proud of our promising rookie nose tackle!

When the snows came and the temperatures dipped, our field of dreams was covered with imaginary ice located in our basement. Ice hockey was our next obsession. I could not swing a hockey stick with any strength, but I cut a formidable figure as a goalie. Again, Billy had the perfect formula to allow me to compete as an equal. He played both offenses and I was in goal. I would have to make three consecutive saves to qualify for a point.

Hockey was not considered just another sport. It was a matter of family pride. Our distant cousin, Stan Mikita, was a perennial all-star center with the Chicago Blackhawks, a team that we followed religiously for years. Although Dad questioned the authenticity of our bloodlines, the fact was that Stan was born in the same village as our paternal grandfather, Jeto. That was more than enough proof for Billy and me to approach hockey as part of our birthright. We had the pleasure of meeting Stan several times after games. He was always gracious, tolerated our worship and once gave us one of his now famous curved hockey sticks. Chicago cheered for Bobby Hull. But in our home, Stan was definitely the man!

Above them all, basketball reigned supreme. This was the sport in which Billy most excelled. That was enough for me. The classroom was my arena; the basketball court was Billy's. He was a natural ball handler and made the assist just as exciting to watch as a jump shot from twenty feet out. With all of his talent and his acclaim in high school, he never forgot that I was his biggest fan and most grateful recipient of those wonderful, soft passes that only he could throw in his lovingly, customized way.

Throughout high school, when he won I had never felt such elation for anyone and never have since. When he lost, I was there to soothe the pain. Although his playing days are over, I frequently reflect on our mutual victories and defeats on the playground and I feel like giving the greatest athlete of my life a standing ovation.

Because of my heightened eye-hand coordination and adroitness at navigating my wheelchair, I excelled at other games as well. I loved to play billiards, ping-pong and miniature golf.

Billy and I were not only rabid participants; we were also avid spectators and students of these games. We collected baseball cards and were equally addicted to sports magazines. To this day, Billy can still recite entire lineups of sporting teams from the 60's and 70's, while spicing his commentary with salient statistics.

Dad did his part to facilitate our great love for sports by escorting us to event after event. We would travel to Pittsburgh for games at Forbes Field, Pitt Field, and the Civic Arena (now affectionately referred to as "the Igloo"). But we also visited Yankee Stadium, Madison Square Garden, and Shea Stadium. We traveled to the Astrodome when it opened. We saw the UCLA Bruins and John Wooden win one of their basketball championships. We visited the Omni in Atlanta to watch Billy's basketball icon, Pistol Pete Maravich. We were at Three Rivers Stadium, when Franco Harris of the Pittsburgh Steelers made "The Immaculate Reception" to beat the Oakland Raiders.

Without a doubt, the two greatest sports' memories are going to the 1972 Summer Olympic Games in Munich and attending the Steelers' last Super Bowl victory at the Rose Bowl for Super Bowl XIV. As for the Olympics, our visit occurred on the first week of the Games and thus my memory is not tainted with the terrorist tragedy of the second week. I shall never forget the night that Billy, Judy and I watched Mark Spitz win three Gold Medals in swimming. To sing our National Anthem among so many people who were not Americans was one of the most patriotic moments of my life. As for the Super Bowl, I was seated in the end zone which enabled me to congratulate "Mean" Joe Greene following the game. He rewarded me with his chinstrap.

When there was nothing to watch, no game to attend, or no opportunity to play outside, Billy would simply invent another game. One of our favorites, was called "Short Yardage." Billy and I would be in our bed and I would be sitting up. Billy would reinforce me with pillows, so that I was stable and balanced. Then he would position other pillows in front of me for further protection.

The object of the game was simple. Billy would play the ball carrier and I was the tackler. To score, meant that Billy needed to plunge over both pillow stacks and me to reach the end zone. Often, because of our zeal, we would both land, arm-in-arm, on the floor. Billy would struggle to get me back into bed before Mom ascended the two stairways that separated her bedroom from ours. I really never cared whether I won any of these games. I simply craved the competition and chance to be with Billy.

Every Saturday night was reserved for televised wrestling! I was introduced to this so-called "sport" by my maternal grandfather, Poppy, who spent most Saturday evenings at our home, while Mom and Dad went on a date. Poppy was more entertaining, than the characters on the television screen. He took it all so seriously, which made it even more comical. I especially loved his Serbian profanities, which Mom never appreciated me recounting the following day.

Sports did not consume all of my boyhood days. We spent time together as a family around the dinner table, whether at home or at a restaurant. Topics of conversation were my father's orthopedic practice, our days at school, current events and frequent lectures from Dad regarding the challenges and obstacles all of us face in life. He extolled the virtues of common sense, honesty, perseverance and self-discipline. Both Mom and he devoted much time in discussing each child's life, talents, and limitations.

Their only expectation was that we would do our best and enjoy doing it. They praised us for our good behavior and expressed their disappointment when we were less than good. Most importantly, they welcomed our opinions and suggestions.

Mom and Dad understood their complimentary roles and performed them with almost perfect execution. There was unanimity on all of the major issues and we knew that. As a result, we could not play one parent off the other. They were consistent and fair. They were also frank and honest. Nothing made me happier than to see the pride and joy on their faces when I succeeded. Conversely, it was particularly painful to fall short of their confidence and trust.

I knew, without exception, how much they adored me and how much my life meant to them. That was a constant source of strength and resolve throughout my early years. My childhood, for the most part, was normal. I lived an active life, like any child who was not disabled. I was punished, even spanked. I learned patience and tolerance. I knew I was loveable and that I was loved. I recall one day succinctly summarizing my childhood perspective to Mom, when I stated: "Mommy, I'm just like everyone else; I just sit all of the time."

Chapter 6

During the summer between kindergarten and first grade, Mom informed me that I would not be returning to McKinley Elementary with the rest of my class. She said that Roosevelt Elementary in another part of town had a special class for children with disabilities and that I was required to attend it. I was extremely disappointed that I was being dislocated from my friends and relocated to another school. This was the first time that I felt the pain of segregation. Although I felt like I was just like everyone else, I was being labeled as disabled first and a first grader second. I was frustrated and angry that I was being treated differently just because I sat in a wheelchair. It just wasn't fair! I didn't have a choice, I had to go to Roosevelt.

It was so painful to leave my familiar surroundings and the supportive network of friends who had made my first educational experience such a success. The fact that I was still able to invite Danny or Mike or Sid over to play on Saturdays was little consolation. I belonged with them, not with a new class of children I didn't know.

I had never associated with children with disabilities. My experience was entirely focused on integrating into an able-bodied world and learning to live in that world and make friends with kids who were not in wheelchairs. This new experience among children like me seemed awkward and not in keeping with the challenges and expectations that Mom and Dad had placed upon me.

They reassured me that I needed to put a positive spin on this new challenge and that it would be a rewarding experience. Mom told me that every new beginning is difficult and intimidating, but that it was also exciting to have the opportunity to meet new people, make new friends and learn new things about their lives and the challenges that they faced with their disabilities.

Soon I realized that Mom and Dad's predictions were absolutely accurate. It was up to me to choose to be happy, no matter what the challenge or trial. My confidence was restored when I realized that I could control my response to this new challenge and that happiness was possible, if I chose it.

The orthopedic class at Roosevelt Elementary was comprised of approximately twelve children from ages 5 to 12 with various disabilities. We received individualized attention and instruction. Darlene and Paula were deaf. Earl had chronic respiratory problems. Suzie was a student with hydrocephalus. Bill had Duchenne Muscular Dystrophy. Madeline used a wheelchair as a result of cerebral palsy.

These classmates were no different from my beloved kindergartners. They laughed. They learned. They lived. And most importantly, they were meeting the challenges of their lives with smiles on their faces and determination in their eyes.

Our teacher, Mrs. Stratton, was talented and creative. In addition to our subjects such as arithmetic, spelling, reading, and science, we would come together several times a week to make crafts. Early on in this process I knew that I was no artist. However, with Mrs. Stratton's help, my creations and projects were fairly impressive. At least, that's what Mom always told me.

There was, however, a major dispute that emerged between Mrs. Stratton and me. It had absolutely nothing to do with the curriculum or her teaching approach. It had everything to do with her rigidity about lunches. This one factor was the only negative aspect of our four years together as student and teacher. Each day my class would be provided with a hot lunch. For the most part, our menu featured many delicious and popular entrees such as hamburgers, sloppy joes, fish sandwiches, fried chicken and swiss steak. However, the vegetable selections were positively awful, at least to my palate!

Mom never cooked anything that we did not love. She did not insist on membership in the "clean plate club" and if she ever did prepare a dish that was not one of our favorites, we could politely decline. Consequently, it was a totally foreign experience for someone to mandate that I was required to eat everything off my plate.

The stress and tension that this created in my life cannot be easily dismissed. I would dread going to school simply because Mrs. Strat-

The Third Opinion

ton would not tolerate green beans, Brussels sprouts or beets remaining on my plate! She didn't care that I had never acquired a taste for any of these vegetables. Neither could she appreciate the fact that I came from an environment that was free of coercion, threats and bribes in order to modify behavior.

When Mom informed me that I could not avoid going to school simply because of my aversion to vegetables, I developed another means to beat Mrs. Stratton at her game. Usually, a baked potato would accompany the vegetable selection. I would eat my potato first and use the skin as an effective camouflage under which I would hide the loathsome beans or beets. The enemy never discovered my effective strategy!

Although I was separated from my kindergarten friends, I learned more about the meaning of life from my new friends. Many of them were not as fortunate as I. Some came from single parent homes. Others did not have brothers and sisters to entertain them during long and lonely weekends. Still others struggled academically.

I was struck by the simple notion that all of us must confront challenges and face our limitations with courage, dignity and resilience. I often sat in amazement to see the effort that these fellow students would expend to complete assignments that seemed so natural and automatic for me. But the student whom I most admired was a diminutive six-year-old with spina bifida. She was feisty, tempestuous, and brilliant. Her name, appropriately enough, was Madonna. She was every bit the show stopper as the other Madonna.

That wasn't the only irony contained in this special class of special students. The name of my new school was Roosevelt Elementary. The legacy of FDR accompanied me to school. I was taught many fundamentals that were embodied in those photographs that Mom and Dad had shown me prior to going to school. It was much more than such rudiments as math and science and English. I was learning much more elementary things than my peers in the "normal" classroom. For that reason, I do not regret any of the time we spent together for the next four years.

Before I was to begin the fifth grade, Mom informed me that the special class was being transferred to a new elementary school which was entirely accessible for students with disabilities. This new school had been constructed on the site of my old school, McKinley Elementary! I would be reunited with my kindergarten classmates after Mrs.

Stratton decided to "mainstream" me long before that term became an integral part of America's special education programs. I was delighted by both of these new developments but disappointed that I was the only student among my new special friends who was invited to return to a "normal" classroom.

Not only was I welcomed back with open arms by my previous friends, I was included within the most popular clique within the class of 30 students. Danny was there, as were Mike, Sid, Nino, and David. We were all extremely competitive and vied for the top grade in every subject.

Besides this dedicated cadre of boys, I began noticing the girls. They seemed to be getting prettier every day. One particular girl became my obsession. Her name was Mary DeLeonardis. She was as alluring and sexy as her name suggests. She is the closest I'll ever come to Sophia Loren. She was not only the brightest student in the class, but the prettiest. I merely had to look into her beautiful green eyes to realize that growing up did have its pleasures.

Unlike kindergarten, I accompanied my classmates on the playground during the fifth and sixth grades. Rather than being separated from them, I was an active participant in most of their games, such as softball and battle ball. On those occasions, when the class would be divided into two different teams, I was always among the first choices, due to my popularity with my classmates. Performance-wise, I was not nearly as successful as I was at home, when Billy would modify the rules. The peer acceptance that I received from simply being selected was compensation enough.

There were some games that I could not play, but I still had a role. During elementary league basketball games I was recruited to be my team's scorekeeper. This assignment was not only much more difficult than I assumed, but totally unnerving. I was determined to overcome this challenge. Much to my disappointment, as well as my team's, I never did.

In one game, McKinley Elementary was playing Lincoln Elementary and I was keeping score, or at least trying to. The game was low scoring and close. At the end, McKinley lost by only two points, and we went home dejected. The next morning, the coach's son delivered the terrible news that McKinley Elementary had actually won the game! I had miscalculated the two teams' total scores. We lost because of me!

The Third Opinion

I felt completely helpless and absolutely worthless. I had let everyone down. Numbers had never been one of my strengths and in my haste to be included among my friends, I had taken on a weightier assignment than I could mentally carry out. The pain and disappointment passed, but I needed to learn that I did not excel at everything that did not require muscle strength. Accounting was another limitation!

My team deserved a competent and accurate scorekeeper, so I issued my resignation and retired to the sidelines to assume a position that was much more compatible with my talents, that of a cheerleader, motivator and sports critic/analyst. I loved the great suspense and waves of emotion that would sweep over me and the rest of the crowd. Keeping score sounded so sterile by comparison, and I didn't miss it.

Like my classmates, I also was growing and maturing physically. However, my weight gain between the ages of 8 and 12 was alarming and quickly threatening my health and life. At the time of my twelfth birthday, I already weighed 140 pounds.

Corresponding to this rapid weight gain, my spine began an equally swift deterioration. Both Dad and my physician in Cleveland, Dr. Paul Vignos, explained that I was developing scoliosis and something had to be done to reverse the curvature of my spine. It wasn't straight. It was growing in different directions and resembled the letter "S."

In an attempt to correct it, I was fitted with a corset — a back brace that featured an array of straps and staves. Although I wore the corset for three years, it had practically no effect on my spine. No matter how much Mom tightened it, as soon as I would take it off to go to sleep at night, my spine would return to its abnormal position.

Besides being ineffective, the corset was extremely cumbersome and maddeningly painful. It was either too high or too low, too tight or too loose. The staves would constantly pinch into my legs, my stomach and tailbone.

No matter what we did, I could never get comfortable for long periods. Compounding this physical torture was the realization that the corset was just not helping. I became very skeptical about its usefulness.

Every time we would travel to Cleveland to visit with Dr. Vignos, I was greeted with a barrage of pessimism and criticism. It was never good news. Dr. Vignos chided me about my weight and inability to lose it. My spine was still crooked. The contractures in my elbows, knees and hips were still there because I was sitting in my wheelchair all the time. They were not worsening, but they were not improving. This news was particularly depressing in light of the fact that I was receiving frequent physical therapy at both home and school.

Therapy was a constant source of aggravation and frustration. When my contractures were stretched, it caused pain, sharp and hot pain, especially in my hamstrings. Mom steadfastly refused to assist with any of my stretching or range-of-motion exercises. She could not even be in the same room when I was receiving therapy. She said it was because she could not bear seeing my grimaces and winces. She also could not tolerate hearing my pleas to "go easy" and not apply as much pressure.

Despite the pain and discomfort that it caused both of us, Mom said that therapy was absolutely imperative. Since I was sitting for longer periods than able-bodied people, she explained that my legs and arms could not extend to their normal degree. Therapy could not strengthen my progressively weakening muscles, no matter what I did or how many times I did it. Ultimately, my voluntary muscles would atrophy. Thus, the purpose behind therapy was to delay the inevitability of my deterioration. I had to do it to try and maintain my strength and flexibility, knowing that I could never get any stronger.

Coupled with these frustrations, I was very concerned about my weight gain. As with my contractures and spine, we tried a lot of different things. Food has always been one of my life's greatest pleasures as well as my family's. Rather than going on bike rides or going hiking like other families, we went to restaurants and enjoyed one another around a meal table.

I wasn't overeating. I could not burn off calories at the rate that an able-bodied person could. Mom and Dad tried a host of diets during these years, but to no avail.

Like my contractures and spine, I could not control my weight. It tormented me. I was so heavy that certain clothes and styles were unavailable because of my size. I was relegated to selecting drab colors that were reserved for "husky" sizes. I had to wear mostly grays and blues in both slacks and sports coats. How I wished that I wasn't so heavy.

I didn't feel that I was good-looking. It wasn't because of my

The Third Opinion

wheelchair or my disability. I was fat and I knew that girls, like Mary, would not be attracted to me if I were fat. My friend Danny and the other popular boys in my class were athletic, muscular and slim. I was none of these.

I always took pride in how I looked. I was not only conscious of my appearance, but had always known that I was being judged by a physically conscious society. To be overweight and disabled in such a society was overwhelming to me. It was just too much to handle. I didn't feel like I could carry both burdens for very long. My self-confidence suffered.

Again, my parents offered their perspectives on my weight problem. Dad explained that some children with muscle diseases had the propensity to put on weight. He said that was part of the disease and there wasn't much that anyone could do to halt or reverse the trend towards obesity. That analysis only increased my feelings of frustration and desperation. I simply could not lose weight. I was destined to be fat!

Mom reassured me that I was handsome, but I knew that she was being more maternalistic than realistic. I wanted so much to believe her, but I could not. Mirrors never lie except at carnivals; sometimes Moms do just to soften the blow.

What meant more to me was the fact that Mom also battled with weight problems for most of her life, following her childbearing years. In that sense, we shared the same challenge. We wanted the same thing — to be thin. She described it as her "constant struggle."

She would deny herself certain foods. She would attempt what seemed to be every new-fangled diet. And, like me, she would weary of trying, fighting and hoping against the odds. Then, when she had beaten herself up for her inability to lose weight, she would begin eating again. And I would join her.

Dad was a different story when it came to my weight problem. He was disciplined and extremely active. Most of all, he was unforgivingly thin. He had lost 45 pounds in two years. He said it was easy. His formula was again characteristically simple: stop eating so much and exercise more often.

He had done the same when it came to smoking cigarettes. Until the day Judy was born and pronounced healthy by the physician, he had smoked two or three packs a day. But on June 16, 1958, he never smoked again. He made his decision to quit and combined it with the perseverance to follow through. No transitional period. No relapses. No excuses. No more cigarettes. I guess he liked the taste of "cold turkey."

His success was downright aggravating. His simple formula was impossible for me to achieve. Physical therapy with its stretching and passive range-of-motion exercises was no match for his beloved Royal Canadian Air Force exercises. Most importantly, he was able to perspire. I never did when I received therapy.

Even when I was playing outside during the summers, I could never muster a sweat. I wished that I could do something, anything that would induce droplets to fall from my forehead. I was so covetous of the ability to perspire that I would dowse my face with water on some afternoons just to look the part. But my counterfeit sweat would immediately evaporate, and so would my dream of ever being thin.

Concern over my expanding waistline was eclipsed by the worry over my crooked spine. Something had to be done. My scoliosis was endangering my health and was already curtailing my activity because of my diminished energy level. Because of the spine's curvature, my rib cage began a corresponding rotation that had a detrimental effect on my lungs. My breathing was restricted and it was hard for me to catch my breath on some days. I was fatigued and required longer rest periods when I returned home from school. I felt weaker generally.

There was another disturbing development. Because of my twisting spine, my pelvis was unbalanced, which meant that my right hip was dislodging from the socket. Both Dad and Dr. Vignos said we had to watch it to make sure that it didn't worsen. I knew that "watch it" meant that the hip would not get any better. After all, they had also been "watching" my back and my weight.

They watched me until the spring of 1968. Then they abandoned their conservative approach, which had only bought time. Aggressive intervention was needed to counter the grave consequences of my deteriorating condition. Talk of back surgery surfaced and it scared me. Not since I was an infant had I been operated on. Those surgeries, however, were exploratory and insignificant muscle biopsies in hopes of obtaining a specific diagnosis. I didn't remember them. This time, surgery would not only be significant, but radical.

The plan was to perform a spinal fusion. An 18-inch steel rod would be fastened onto certain vertebra and then reinforced by horse

The Third Opinion

bone to straighten my back. Straightening a spine takes time. I would be asleep for at least five hours. When I woke up, I would be in a cast, a terrifyingly large cast! Dad called it a hip-spica and his description sounded downright bizarre!

Not only would I be forced to wear this cast for six months, it would not allow me to sit upright for that period. At my age, that sounded a lot like forever. I was absolutely traumatized by this new information and I cried most of the two and one-half hours traveling from Dr. Vignos' office in Cleveland to our home in Steubenville.

Dad had great confidence in the orthopedic surgeon, who would be performing the surgery, Dr. Charles Herndon. Unlike Vignos, Herndon was warm and approachable.

Both Dr. Herndon and Dr. Vignos were less confident of my ability to survive the surgery. Their questions centered principally on my lungs. My respiratory system was comparatively weak. There was a chance therefore, a real possibility, that I would die on the table. I cowered, Mom flinched, and Dad was momentarily dazed. I was only twelve years old and facing two cruel choices.

The first was to remain on the course that we had taken for the last three years. Cautious and conservative. Things would only get worse if I chose this option. My spine would curve more and my quality of life would be decreased. I would sit for fewer hours as the years passed. My breathing capacity would become more compromised and I would look deformed and lurch to one side. My hip would eventually dislocate and need repair. This option as a result did not appear very attractive. My life would be short and increasingly inactive. I would be required to spend more time in bed to conserve my strength. Not much of an option. The second held no guarantees either. The risks were every bit as frightening. Dad explained that usually such radical surgery was performed on teenagers who were at least fifteen years old and able-bodied. They also had healthy lungs that had not grown weaker over the years like mine. He said that the physicians did not know of anyone who had been as young or as disabled as I was who had undergone such surgery. I felt like a medical guinea pig. My young age was not the problem. My atrophying lungs were. And if I survived the surgery, the rehabilitation time seemed every bit as daunting.

The body cast would be removed after six months and replaced with a sitting cast. That would also be on for six months. The surgery would be performed during the summer, but that meant I would not be able to start the seventh grade with my friends.

After convalescing at the hospital in Cleveland following surgery, I would be transported to the Rainbow Clinic, a rehabilitation center on the outskirts of Cleveland. I would remain there for six months and then be allowed to go home. Home was 125 miles away and life as I knew it was going to be even farther away than that. I would be separated from family and friends and fun. I would be segregated from the rest of my world. But most importantly, I didn't want to die on the operating table. There was too much for me left to do. I thought about going to college and having a career and getting married. I was not even a teenager yet. I was being forced to choose between a life that would eventually kill me or a surgery that might. I was living a nightmare and I couldn't wake up!

If I survived the surgery and tolerated the year-long rehabilitation, Dad said that I would be healthier and live longer. He stated, "Son, we have to take this risk. If we don't, you will only get worse and die. A spinal fusion is our only hope of you living a long time. I know it's scary, but we have to do it. You are going to be better off. Remember you are a fighter and you are going to be okay. Mommy and Daddy are going to be there and when I can't be, Mom will be there for you and I will bring Carole, Billy and Judy to see you on the weekends."

I hung onto every word. But the word "fighter" was the one that made the decision. That was the one word that made the difference. That is who I was. I wasn't going to stop fighting just because there was a possibility that I would not survive this battle.

I had survived others and surpassed the expectations of other physicians and their predictions about my longevity on earth. I had already beaten the odds. That's one thing the doctors didn't know about me, but Mom and Dad did. When people counted me out, I had gotten off the canvass to fight another round. I was a fighter. I loved the competition. I loved being an underdog.

This is what I did and did well. The surgery was just another opponent that underestimated my endurance and resolve to live. The decision was made before we arrived home. With my family behind me, I didn't feel so alone. I needed to be brave and to accept this next challenge. Having faith in the physicians, in myself, and in God. It was time to jump back into the ring and fight for my life.

Chapter 7

I was admitted into Hanna House, part of Case Western University Medical Center in Cleveland, one week before the scheduled surgery on July 31, 1968. Dad said that they wanted to give me time to get used to these new surroundings and to "work me up" for the surgery. I interpreted that as a time of preparation and observation before the operation.

The first few days were surprisingly enjoyable. I was receiving a lot of attention from orthopedic residents and the nursing staff. I underwent a battery of tests to ascertain how strong my lung capacity really was. These tests were challenging and exhausting. I would have to force air through a number of sophisticated apparatuses that would print out my results on graphs. These tests struck me as being very athletic and tailored to what I perceived as one of my talents — holding my breath for long periods of time and developing strong lungs.

My confidence stemmed from the fact that I could hold my breath under water for extended periods of time. Because I could not compete with other kids at the swimming pool by either swimming, diving or engaging in chicken fights, I had to find another means through which I could make friends and offer them another form of competition. Consequently, I would challenge children to holding-your-breath contests in which I was always victorious.

Mom got nervous every time I would plunge my head into the water and float lifelessly for a minute and one-half to two minutes. In my life preserver, I had the ability to turn over on my back when I needed to catch a breath. This ability to excel at just one thing in the swimming pool made it a lot easier when my friends could not play with me.

Another reason for my confidence in my lungs was because of my love for singing. Since I was eight years old, I had been a member of the St. Paul's Episcopal Church Choir of men and boys. Although my family attended St. Paul's, the choir director recruited talented voices from grade schools and other churches and singing organizations. Thus, we were quite an ecumenical ensemble that practiced several evenings a week. The choir was famous, in large part, for its boys' soprano section. I was a great boy soprano before puberty struck! I missed singing the melody lines of many beautiful hymns and anthems. I felt too young to sing the baritone line with the group of 40 and 50-year-olds who comprised that section of our choir.

Despite these accomplishments, everyone at Hanna House was concerned about my lungs. I never learned the results of all of the breathing tests, but I assumed that I had done all right because my spinal fusion wasn't delayed.

My fun in the hospital ended the day Dr. Herndon told me that I would be fitted for my hip spica cast and would wear it until the day before surgery. Nothing could have prepared me for what was to come, not even Mom.

I tried to be brave, but tears began flowing as soon as the hot plaster of Paris was wrapped around practically my entire body in a mummy-like fashion.

I remember being surrounded by a very helpful and sensitive team of people who made sure that I didn't fall off the rack-like contraption that I was lying on.

When this process was over, I resembled something akin to a human turtle. The cast began at the top of my head and covered my entire chest and back, with openings for my arms. But it didn't end there. It covered my hips and pelvis down to my knees with a twelve-inch rod separating my knees with openings to allow me to go to the bathroom.

It was as uncomfortable as it looked. It would be my home — my prison for the next six months. This was going to be so much more difficult than I ever expected. Both Mom and Dad had done their best to prepare me with the limited information made available to them. The physicians and hospital staff did not know how I would react to the cast because they did not know me as a person. I was merely a

The Third Opinion

patient to them. Thus, the horror and shock surrounding my cast were magnified by the feeling that I was so alone.

I felt utterly abandoned while in the casting room, despite the fact that the people surrounding me provided reassuring words and tender caresses during the procedure. Nonetheless, I felt violated and humiliated. With each new layer of plaster, I felt like I was losing part of who I was. I was just a twelve year old kid who sat all of the time, loved people and loved his life. The cast was evidence, clear and convincing evidence, that I was different. I needed to accept the fact that because of my disability I would be required to change my course, to adapt to this next phase and to do it virtually alone. I was in uncharted waters and unsure of my ability to sail through this storm. I was very fearful that I would be unable to endure it.

When I was taken back to my room, Mom was there, forcing a grin and fighting back tears. After I was transferred back into my bed from the gurney, we both cried. I realized this was new for her, too. She also was afraid and uncertain of the future. Both of us were being asked to adjust to a new life, one that we had been spared since my infancy. We had not spent any time in a hospital since I was eighteen-months-old at the NIH. Both of our lives were changing.

What made this so terrifying was that I knew that this was only the beginning of a very long, hazardous road. Rather than worrying about what would come next, I needed to direct my attention to what I could control — my feelings, thoughts and dreams. There would be surprises and horrors along the way. And it was obvious that I had not done enough work before reaching this point. I was not prepared emotionally, psychologically or spiritually.

Mom directed my focus to what was inside me in order to make sense of the shell of plaster that was outside me. Our relationship was changing. Not only were we mother and son, but also teacher and student, psychologist and client, priest and penitent, coach and player. My childhood world of fun and innocence ended. Mom was my beacon to bring me back from the darkness of my plaster prison.

Her tears let me know that I mattered. Her ears let me know that my fears were heard. She encouraged me to tell her how I felt while the cast was being put on me. I told her that my back really hurt when they tugged and pulled on me while applying the plaster. I told her how scared I was when they started covering my neck and the back of my head. It was hard to breathe and I feared that I might suffocate. I told her I wanted to go home.

She listened intently. She empathized totally. She told me that I must feel terribly afraid and very alone. She then said, "You're my brave boy and we're going to get through this. I know how hard it must be, but Mommy knows how strong you are. Your father and I are very proud of you." Feeling like giving up was a natural reaction. But actually giving up wasn't me. It certainly would not be the last time that she would need to remind and in turn define me.

She then described the cast in great detail. She told me how it looked, how long it was, how thick it was and where the openings were. Her intention was clear. We both needed to understand our new opponent and therefore the unknown became knowable. We then could establish a plan to combat this next challenge.

Even the mundane and commonplace routines of life were gone. I had to learn how to live from a supine position. First, I had to be fed by someone. I had never depended on anyone to feed me. That is one thing I could do the same as anyone else. Chewing and swallowing were much slower and much more risky lying on my back. When someone other than Mom would feed me, I always felt pressured for time. They didn't have to say it, but I perceived that the nurses felt imposed upon and that their other patients had more significant "medical" needs.

Enjoying a bowl of soup was strictly off limits. Because of the awkward angles between the spoon and my mouth, I would end up having to slurp the broth without getting the rest of the contents or have the entire spoonful spill down my face and into my cast. It just was not worth the hassle.

Brushing my teeth was another obstacle. I could no longer brush independently and required assistance. Again, as with eating, everyone who brushed them, employed their personal technique, not mine. They either did it too strenuously or too softly. When it came time to discharge the toothpaste from my mouth, I needed to learn the versatility of a straw.

Before spitting out the toothpaste, I learned to suck water into my mouth from a cup and then by placing the straw into another basin or cup I would expel toothpaste, water and saliva. It took some control but it was easier than it sounds, albeit an unappetizing exercise in hygienics.

Watching television created another adventure in improvisation.

The Third Opinion

To see the television, which was placed on the opposite end of my room, I was given a pair of oddly configured glasses called "prism" glasses. By employing a double mirror, these glasses enabled me to see directly in front while looking towards the ceiling. They were not as neat or obnoxious as 3-D glasses, but I thought they were pretty avant-garde.

Without a doubt, the biggest challenge and clearly the most humiliating was using a bedpan. Until this point in my life, I had simply been lifted on the commode to defecate. I had used a urinal for years, which impressed me as convenient and private. But using a bedpan was disgusting.

Due to the limited opening provided by the cast, I could not use a traditional bedpan, which closely resembles the top of a toilet seat. Instead, I was given a "fracture" pan which was one-half the size of a bedpan and extremely shallow. It looked like a miniature plastic drawer and to sit atop it was no small feat, not to mention, uncomfortable. To think of using this makeshift toy toilet was absolutely anathema to me!

Naturally, I became constipated and was subjected to the additional assault of an enema, one day before surgery. Now, well beyond the limits of privacy and decorum, I finally succumbed, only to be visited with the ultimate indignity of sitting in my excrement until a nurse would clean me with an endless array of rough washcloths.

I never got used to the mess or the lack of privacy of it all. I detested using it then and during subsequent hospitalizations. The anxiety and stress of bowel care in the hospital has never been reduced. Indeed, I became so preoccupied about the critical need for regularity, that the ultimate success of any hospital day turned on whether or not I had a successful bowel movement. No matter how hard it is to recount or read about later, nothing in my hospitalizations threatened my stability and esteem more. I never got used to it. There are some aspects of my life that remain permanent struggles.

For a moment, however, life got easier. One day before the surgery Dr. Herndon said that they would remove my body cast. It was only one day, but my feeling of liberation was worth it. Even knowing that tomorrow would begin a longer and more painful ordeal than I had ever previously experienced in my life, I still had one day to sit in my wheelchair and enjoy my body with its old supple spine.

In some respects, it was a return to the life before I had arrived at the hospital. I felt like a boy again, and not a largely anonymous hospital patient or medical experiment. It was really difficult to face the prospects, the unknown prospects, of my future that would begin the next day. It was a future that I feared might never come because of my weak lungs. Many times during that last day I told Mom I just wanted to go home and enjoy life as I had. I wished that I didn't have to go through with the surgery. In short, I was terrified of dying.

As always, Mom joined her tears with mine. That always made me feel less alone and validated my concerns. It was okay to be afraid at times during our lives, she explained. Life was full of trials and challenges that were intimidating and scary. This was one such trial. It was a big one for both of us.

Although this was a significant challenge with equally significant risks, we had to have faith that God would sustain me through this next ordeal. She reminded me how talented Dr. Herndon was and that my lungs were actually stronger than anyone was willing to acknowledge. She then said, "There are so many things left for you to do in this life. God has not brought you this far to fail. There is a purpose for your life, otherwise, you would have already been taken from us at an earlier age, as the doctors had predicted."

She recounted the story of FDR when he had contracted polio. Contemplating his future, FDR had told his wife that he feared trying because he didn't want to fail. Eleanor told him, "Then don't fail." This was a similar moment of truth for me. I didn't want to die. I didn't want to fail.

We began planning for the immediate future. Earlier that year someone had given me a soft, silver crucifix that I treasured. I told Mom that when she and Dad came into the recovery room the next day, I wanted her to bring that special crucifix. I knew that I would be pretty groggy. Nevertheless, I asked her to hold the crucifix in front of my eyes and I would flash her a "V" for victory sign to reassure her that I was okay.

As evening fell, so did my spirits. Mom and Dad had to leave, but I didn't want them to, especially on this night. They would be back tomorrow, they said, and I needed to prepare for surgery. Dad said they would give me some medication to help me sleep. The morning would begin earlier than I was used to.

Before they left, Mom suggested that we pray for help and success. It

The Third Opinion

wasn't a rote prayer, but one of her customary, extemporaneous ones in which she expressed gratitude and thanksgiving for the health and prosperity that we as a family had always enjoyed. She thanked God for me and the blessing that I had been to my parents, siblings and friends. She told God that He had helped me during other hard times and also helped her. She explained that we needed His help again and so did the doctors and nurses who would be assisting in the surgery the next day. She asked Him, to strengthen me and protect me during the operation when she and Dad would be separated from me. Before she closed, she again thanked God for the privilege of being my mother and for bringing me into her life and for all the experiences that we had shared together as mother and child.

When her prayer had ended, she flashed her radiant smile and promised me that everything was going to be all right and that I must have faith in God, the doctors and her prayer. Dad then kissed my forehead, and as he had done during previous difficult moments, said, in a Slovak term of endearment, "Ne plach, bebo," which means, "Don't cry, baby."

He told me, "We're proud of you, son. Everything is going to be okay." They left and I lay in the darkness with my tears and my fears.

Before too long, an orderly appeared with several razors to shave my back, legs, hips, chest and stomach as well as my groin. I was intrigued by this process and drew a comparison to what Olympic swimmers do with their bodies prior to a competition. He was very gentle and his presence and touch were comforting.

I was soon alone to contemplate deeper questions than Olympic-size swimming pools. The feelings of desperation and isolation reappeared and were compounded by the fact that my roommate had been asleep, a profoundly deep sleep, for at least two or three hours. I envied his peacefulness and resented his loud snoring that offered an obnoxious counterpoint to my quiet agony a few feet away. I felt so alone. I needed some way to pierce my loneliness and terror. I had cried enough and my worrying was escalating as the minutes ticked on. Mom had offered her prayer, but now it was my turn.

I told God how afraid I was about dying the next day. I needed to know whether I would survive the surgery. I needed something more than a parental hug or verbal reassurances. Put simply, I was seeking a sign. I asked God that if everything was going to be okay, that He simply cause my slumbering roommate to turn over or cough or make some movement to give me an indication that all would go well the next day. I knew I was asking a lot because my roommate had not moved since he had fallen asleep.

Ten seconds after I had offered my prayer, my roommate sat bolt upright in his bed, fully awake and turned to me and said, "Stevie, if you need anything during the night, I will be here." I thanked him for his gracious and generous offer. He then immediately resumed his previous posture and I rejoiced in this revelation, knowing that Dr. Herndon and I would have some heavenly assistance the next day! Snoring has never been more beautiful than on that night in a quiet, lonely hospital room in Cleveland, Ohio. I was ready to face the music.

Chapter 8

As I squinted through the haze of anesthesia, I knew that the surgery was over and I had survived it. I could make out the figures of my parents standing next to my bed under the bright lights of the recovery room. I sensed Mom's urgency for us to communicate. She was smiling brightly and displaying the silver crucifix. She asked whether I could see it. Of course, I could. What I was unable to do was to form my fingers in a V-shape to signal to her that I was okay, according to our pre-operation agreement. In fact, I believed that I made the victory sign several times for her, but the heaviness of the anesthesia was still separating me from reality.

I also noticed that Mom and Dad were standing unusually close to each other in their hospital gowns. Dad seemed to be holding Mom up. I learned later that Mom nearly collapsed and fainted when they first entered the recovery room and saw me lying on the gurney. My face, hospital gown and sheets were still bloodstained, which had traumatized Mom.

I had been through quite a battle in the surgical suite and my appearance confirmed it. The surgery took longer than expected — six and a half hours instead of five. I lost quite a bit of blood — six pints.

The good news was that the Harrington rod was now in place beside my spine. A new hip spica cast once again covered me, and my delicate lungs had performed admirably. Dad was visibly relieved and said, "You look great. Dr. Herndon said everything was fine during the surgery. Just try to get some rest. We're not going to go anywhere and we'll see you later in the surgical intensive care unit."

I knew that intensive care was for people who were in critical condition, but I felt that I wasn't critical and that I was just being taken there as precaution. I was not connected to any monitors or respirators. I was breathing on my own with the help of a little oxygen through my nose.

However, I was extremely nauseated and truly wished that I could turn on my side rather than lie on my back. Also, I was frustrated by the fact that I could not communicate clearly or forcefully enough to get my wishes granted. I felt like the nursing staff was virtually ignoring me and were too preoccupied with the needs of other patients in the room. When helpers did arrive, they were loud and abrasive.

Thankfully, I didn't remain in the recovery room for very long. I was transferred to the intensive care unit where it was quiet, peaceful and dimly lit. I tried to sleep, but the overwhelming pain that enveloped my entire body made that impossible.

I was astonished at how I felt. It hurt so much that it was hard to breathe. When Mom and Dad reappeared, I told Mom that it felt as if I had just been run over by a train. She said that it must be awful and that she wished it didn't hurt so much.

My nausea subsided and the staff's attentiveness vastly improved in intensive care. Unlike their colleagues in the recovery room, these nurses were kind and sensitive. I felt safer there than I had in days, maybe weeks. But I was so thirsty. I repeatedly asked for water. I was politely told that drinking a cup of water at this stage was premature and would only cause a return of the nausea. The nurse said that it was a good sign that I was thirsty.

Soon thereafter, they brought cold, soaked wash rags for me to suck on and then they gave me the day's ultimate delicacy — ice chips. Nothing so basic ever tasted so good! Because of the delirium of my pain, I was content to remain in intensive care for one night with my brand new industrial-strength spine.

The next day, I had improved to the extent that I was allowed to return to my room. But it seemed as if I was never going to get there. The route that we traveled from intensive care seemed to be three miles and three elevators away. What annoyed me the most, however, was that every time that we would roll over a crack in the floor or a door threshold, there would be a terrific bolt of pain pounding my body and teasing my sanity. When we finally arrived in the room, I declared to Mom that I had been brought back via the Pennsylvania turnpike, which Dad had always condemned for its unmerciful curves and chronically cracked asphalt.

Mom applauded my sarcasm. She was glad that the surgery had not changed my sense of humor. She said, "I can see you're getting better. You've got your fight back."

Dr. Herndon, however, was furious, not with me, but with the nursing staff in the intensive care unit. He came unglued when he found out that I had not been medicated for over eight hours because the nurses in Intensive Care Unit were waiting for me to ask for it. I didn't know that I was supposed to ask for pain medication. I thought I was supposed to "tough it out."

My convalescent period over the next two weeks was as turbulent as the political situation in America's big cities that summer of '68. Cleveland had not eluded race riots. In August they were encroaching upon the grounds of Case Western Reserve and the medical complex.

Mom would give me hourly updates on the scene outside my fourth floor window. Ohio's governor had called a state of emergency and had enlisted the help of the National Guard to stabilize the area and monitor the simmering situation. Mom could see soldiers, armed jeeps, tanks and klieg lights everywhere.

She told me that she had to leave the hospital before it got dark for at least two weeks. She tried not to worry, but the hot, muggy nights only fueled the bitterness and anger that were percolating from the Cleveland ghettos. I loved and admired her for her courage and independence in the face of trouble. She would honor the evening curfews that had been imposed on the streets, but would return the next day refreshed and totally focused upon my rehabilitation. America would just have to wait.

To address our state of emergency inside the walls of the hospital, Mom enlisted the help of a variety of sources. Her primary strategy as always was complete empathy and optimism. She was never too tired to listen, never dismissive about my concerns and worries. She never minimized my feelings. No matter what, she was there. My constant ally.

She inserted herself into every facet of my life. She respected, however, the fact that I was ultimately the one to pass through this test. She encouraged me to be independent, not co-dependent. She would only intercede with the doctors or nurses after receiving my approval. She realized the critical difference between being a support rather than a crutch. The former fortified me, the latter would have crippled me.

We talked about everything. No subject was taboo. We talked about family, friends and the future, both mine and hers. She candidly expressed her opinions on current events, food, places where she and Dad had visited, her relationship with her parents, her relationship with Dad and my siblings, her religious beliefs and spiritual insights, as well as her community work in securing rights for persons with disabilities in our community and throughout the state of Ohio.

When we were not talking, she would read to me. Her hospital library would include newspapers, magazines, sermons, and other inspirational stories from the Reverend Norman Vincent Peale, the famed author of *The Power of Positive Thinking*, and the Bible, particularly the New Testament.

On occasions, when I was feeling insecure or uncomfortable, I would say, "Mom, tell me about somebody." This meant that I wanted her to direct my attention from my worries and concerns about my present state of being. These stories about the people in our lives would have the effect of energizing me because it caused me to think of times when I was home and healthy, rather than in this distant place.

At other times, when I simply didn't feel like talking or listening, she simply would hold my hand or squeeze it. That fleshy connection always comforted and strengthened me. No one should ever underestimate the power of a mother's touch. Not ever.

Often our discussions and times together were interrupted by my therapists, dietary personnel, laboratory staff, nurses and doctors. When they came, especially Herndon and his platoon of residents, we would have to shift gears quickly. Mom said this was my only opportunity each day to tell Dr. Herndon how I was feeling, really feeling. I recognized that I had to jettison the automatic "fine, thank you" that had been my response as a child. I did that and said that for the audience. It made them feel better. I was a boy in a wheelchair and I was proclaiming my happiness and acceptance.

Now was different. My audience had changed. So had my needs. I was not seeking acceptance or integration into an able-bodied society. In the hospital, I was fighting to restore my health. Most importantly, I could not pretend that I was fine, when in reality I was in almost

The Third Opinion

constant pain. I had to concisely and precisely describe my feelings and my progress or regression. And I didn't have a lot of time.

I knew that orthopedic surgeons were not known for their patience or their appreciation for the spoken word. They were busy, preoccupied people who let their medical talents do their talking. After all, I was being raised by one.

Dad often recounted with great pride how fast he could complete his morning rounds and how both colleagues and patients marveled at his energy and efficiency. Dr. Herndon, although a medical school professor, was cut out of the same mold. He was not interested in idle chit-chat. He was solely interested in my well being from an orthopedic standpoint. I had to adjust as a result.

I was given no more than five minutes every day to ask my questions of him and respond to his. Accordingly, I needed to measure the relative importance of my host of concerns. Some days I would focus Herndon's attention on a particular part of my cast that was causing pressure and pain. Usually, it was the area around my tailbone. Several times a day, I would need to be turned onto my side so that either Mom or a nurse could pry that part of the cast away from my body. Permanent relief was not possible.

On other days, I would tell Herndon that I had failed to have a bowel movement. It upset me that Herndon did not appreciate my degree of urgency. He was non-committal. His response was always the same. "Are you taking your stool softener? If that is not working, we will order some Milk of Magnesia." The stool softeners were not producing regularity and neither would a cup of Milk of Magnesia every two or three days. Herndon's apathy really infuriated me. I tried every nuance and inflection that I could muster to convey the significance of this issue. Herndon was impervious to both my passion and persuasion. Indeed, Herndon's aloof response escalated my anxiety. He was acting and speaking as if it were no big deal. I felt guilty that I was so obsessed about it.

I eventually conceded to Mom that I would only articulate my concerns to her and to the nurses. As for Herndon, I would limit my daily reports to my back and the cast. Dad had taught me well.

But besides teaching me about the short attention spans of orthopedic surgeons, Dad also taught me that everyone working at hospitals — physicians, nurses, L.P.N.'s, orderlies, dieticians, custodial staff was deserving of my respect, courtesy and gratitude. They all contributed to a patient's well being. Unlike most physicians whom I've met, they were less inclined to role-play, more apt to be themselves. They were real people living real lives.

I wanted them to know that I sincerely cared about them. In turn, they would care about me. While they washed, fed and turned me, I interviewed them. I asked about their work schedules — how many days a week they worked, whether they changed shifts, if they worked the grave-yard shift, what were their sleeping habits? What kind of things did they do when they weren't working? What did they like and dislike about their jobs? These questions were designed to break the ice and to humanize this uniformed troop of people. Consequently, many of them served me far beyond the call of duty.

By applying the Golden Rule, many of them demonstrated great concern and interest in not only my medical condition but also my life. I was no ordinary patient to them. They were not faceless to me.

By expressing my interest in and appreciation for them, I was giving something back. I was serving them as a friend, confidant, or sounding board. They might have dressed the same and had similar job descriptions, but each of their hearts and souls were fascinating and unique. I approached everyone as a prospective friend, and thus the hospital and its cold, impersonal ambiance became a warmer, more caring place where true healing took place.

Besides the new friends that I made in the hospital, I kept in touch with my friends at home in Steubenville. I would telephone Danny, Mary, and Mary's cousin, Linda DiFalco, who was already a freshman in high school. Linda almost instantly replaced Mary as my new obsession. I met her on the last day of sixth grade — cleanup day. There were only a handful of us at school to help our teacher, Mrs. Young, close up for the summer.

Linda was positively alluring. Quite a bit shorter than Mary, lighter-skinned, the same exquisite green eyes and a petite but stunningly proportionate figure. What really clinched it, she called me "Stevie." No one had called me "Stevie" since the third grade. Having this experienced, older woman call me "Stevie" was so seductive that I never grew tired of her saying it. I was never her boyfriend and that was frustrating. But I never lost hope that some day she would realize how much I cared. Until that occurred, I was satisfied being her close friend. We spent literally hours on the phone together. Linda did most of the talking, and I was more than content to listen and to

The Third Opinion

idolize my older woman.

In addition to phone calls, I received a barrage of mail. Each afternoon Mom and I eagerly awaited the hospital's mail delivery. Even those whose job it was to deliver the mail were amazed by the sheer volume of correspondence I was receiving. Naturally, there were letters and cards from my classmates and relatives. More surprising was the number of get-well wishes that I received from adult friends of my parents.

I never realized that my life meant so much to them. They expressed such touching sentiments that Mom and I were often brought to tears. Mom said I had a huge network of people who loved and supported me. That realization both inspired and frustrated me. They were at home and I was in the hospital. They were going on with their lives and I was barely hanging on to mine.

They could place a phone call or write a card, but they still could not realize what I was being subjected to. When they hung up the phone or sent the card, their life resumed its normal pace. I felt expendable and realized that no matter how important we think we are, our absence really does not change others' lives for very long. That realization hurt and produced a loneliness that usually hits most of us long after our twelfth birthdays. I longed to go home and return to my prior life. Before I could, though, I would have to spend the next six months at Rainbow Rehabilitation Center.

I knew I wasn't going to like Rainbow. Its name sounded contrived and disingenuously cheery. I feared that it was a place where disabled people were housed and forgotten. Mom said I could tolerate anything for six months. I wasn't so sure.

Realizing that it was a long shot, I asked Herndon if I could remain at Hanna House rather than transfer to Rainbow. I had grown accustomed to the surroundings as well as the staff. With my pain subsiding, I was feeling more comfortable and since I had made friends the thought of leaving was even more unappealing. Herndon rejected my offer.

My fears about Rainbow were confirmed on the day I arrived. In some respects, it was worse that I imagined. Most nightmares are. Naturally, the building itself was foreboding. Red bricks. Overgrown ivy. Yellow fluorescent lights. Long, darkened corridors. Light years away from Herndon's description.

The living quarters were downright appalling. There were no

private or semi-private rooms. Only large, cold, impersonal wards with fifteen beds each. One small, black and white television. Not to mention, tough-talking orderlies who were more like football coaches than nurses.

The other patients were so damn well-adjusted and content with Rainbow, that I was convinced they had been brainwashed. Admittedly, they were more independent than I. Because they were able-bodied and had the use of their arms, they reveled in their ability to lie on their stomachs and wheel themselves around on modified gurneys that featured larger than normal-sized wheels. Not only were these other patients happier and more autonomous, they were older. They were high school age. I was a sixth-grader who drew comfort from my stuffed Snoopy.

I despised everything about Rainbow. I was constantly asking Mom to close the curtains around my bed in order to escape from this environment. Mom grew impatient with my hostility towards Rainbow. She told me I needed to socialize more, isolate less.

But I steadfastly refused to engage anyone, including her. I did not feel like talking or eating or listening. I just wanted to go home or back to Hanna House.

Most days, I couldn't even force a smile. I felt guilty that everyone else seemed so excited to be there. I felt I had been sentenced to death row. When I did speak, it was monotone. I just wanted to sleep away the entire experience or squeeze Mom's hand and cry.

For the first time in my life, I was depressed. Nothing was improving. I wanted to like Rainbow, but I couldn't pull myself out of this ever-deepening well of doom. I had been there for three weeks when the entire family arrived for Labor Day. My Aunt Anna from Erie, Pennsylvania, had prepared a smorgasbord, but I didn't have an appetite. I didn't desire conversation, either. I hated Rainbow and no one concurred. I wanted only to be left alone with my dissent.

I identified with the Czechoslovakian people who had revolted against the tyranny of Communism during that same period. They had brazenly challenged Soviet authority and demanded the adoption of democratic reforms. I empathized with their frustration and rage directed toward the Soviet monolith. I admired their courage and bravery when the Soviet tanks began to thwart this brief, heroic uprising. With relatives still living behind the Iron Curtain, in Czechoslovakia and Yugoslavia, Dad and Mom closely watched this revolution. This was the only topic that slightly interested me that Labor Day in 1968, when we picnicked under the big tree in Rainbow's courtyard.

Dad sensed that day that I was losing my fight and my positive attitude. Two days later, he telephoned Mom and said he had talked to Dr. Herndon about my mental health. He requested that he be allowed to take me home to Steubenville. Dad told Herndon that he had already arranged for an electric hospital bed to be moved into our family room and that my Jamaican attendant, Ronnie, could meet my nursing needs. Herndon approved; I was going home!

I was ecstatic. I smiled and laughed for the first time in too long as I watched Rainbow disappear from the back window of the ambulance that was taking me back to family, friends and to the kind of person I knew I was. Sure, I was wearing a cast. But it only covered, not changed, my heart.

Chapter 9

Besides providing for my personal daily care, the issue of my education became paramount. My junior high school, Harding, was inaccessible and thus it appeared that I would be consigned to being tutored at home. This option was not a very attractive one because I would be segregated from my classmates. Mom explored alternatives.

She discovered a stimulating option. I could participate in all of my classes and not leave the house. I would attend school with the help of an intercom that required a student to carry a transmitter from class to class that would air the proceedings to my receiver at home. I was able to answer questions and engage in class discussions simply by pressing a button. It truly was "the next best thing to being there."

To take notes and have my arms free to press the intercom, I needed to be transferred each morning from my bed to a hospital gurney via lift. This was quite a hair-raising experience! After being 'bathed in bed', which entailed having my face and limbs washed, I would be turned on my left side so that a plastic sling could be placed underneath me. Once I was secure in the sling, then the lift would raise me above the bed.

The lift would then lower me onto the gurney after I dangled in the air for a couple of minutes. Then I would be turned on my stomach and scooted forward to hang over the edge so that I could work at my desk. To prevent me from falling over the edge several belts would be tied around both me and the gurney to hold me in place.

I was unable to hold my head upright and so I used a headband to prevent my head from falling to my chest. Since it only supported my forehead, gravity played havoc with my jaw which exacerbated my temporal mandibular joint syndrome that weakened and closed my jaw.

Living life horizontally had its drawbacks. I never felt completely clean. Showers and baths were impossible. The exposed parts of my body could be washed daily with a wash cloth, but so much of me was encased that I always felt dirty and oily.

Hair care was equally difficult and frustrating. Since access to the back of my head was restricted by the cast, shampoos were infrequent, yet elaborate productions. With plastic sheets, buckets and other assorted containers, each week I would hang over the end of the gurney to have Mom or my attendant, Ronnie, scrub my hair. To have my hair cleaned and my scalp stimulated was sheer ecstasy! The whole procedure was time-consuming, messy and dangerous. But so worthwhile. I felt more like myself following those glorious shampoos than I did at any other time during those six months I was in my cast.

No one knew how to comb my hair properly, but that was immaterial. I still wanted to look good no matter how few people came to visit and how quickly my clean hair would become tangled and unkempt.

I left the house only three times during that period — twice to attend Steubenville Big Red High School's football games. I had been attending Big Red games for years. They were electrifying occasions. It was as if the entire town turned out.

Dad, being the only orthopedic surgeon in Steubenville, was well known and popular. Consequently, it seemed as though everyone knew me, too.

In those days there was no wheelchair accessible seating in the stands, so we sat on the sidelines. I felt a little insecure and vulnerable each time a play was run to our side, but Billy and Dad were there to protect me along with Steubenville's Chief of Police, George Mavromatis — a man who hardly ever smiled but who never wandered from me for fear that I would not be shielded from a player running out-of-bounds.

High school football was an integral part of my town's identity. Steubenville was not divided along ethnic, racial, or socioeconomic lines. Instead, the only factor that separated one segment of society from another was whether you cheered for the city's public high school, Steubenville Big Red, or the private high school, Catholic Central.

I have never witnessed a fiercer rivalry at any level of sports, including college and professional. When the two teams met each year, the passions and dreams of our community spilled onto the field. Everyone worked hard in my hometown and their kids played just as hard on that last Friday night in November.

Eating, just like personal hygiene, was another challenge during my rehabilitation. Chewing, swallowing, and digesting food required more time, effort, and patience. I had to be fed at every meal which was particularly annoying. Usually, Mom or Ronnie would be my designated feeder. Meals ceased to be fun and were reduced to nothing more than a necessary part of my regimen.

Each meal reminded me of how different and restrictive my life had become. Relying on someone else, I could not eat at the regular pace that I was accustomed to when I fed myself. The fork would come to me either too quickly or too slowly. I had to wait my turn. One bite for me; the next bite for them.

Most of all, I missed the lively discussions that highlighted my family's evening meals. Now, the simple mechanics of eating superseded everything else. Meals were something I was forced to do, not what I enjoyed doing.

I missed the company of my family around the dinner table, which had become the hallmark of our family togetherness. While Ronnie fed me in the converted family/hospital room, I could hear both the clatter and chatter of dinner from the kitchen forty feet away, but inaccessible to me as a result of one narrowly-cut corner. My motorized wheelchair could negotiate this turn, but my gurney couldn't. As a result, I was relegated to my room and felt the pain each evening of being a stranger in my own home. I asked Ronnie to turn on the television, not to watch it, but to block out the irritating din of a happy meal. My family was enjoying themselves and I wasn't. That never tastes good.

The third time that I ventured out of the house was for Thanksgiving. I was not required to travel very far — only about sixty feet. After fully opening the picture window in our family room, Dad, Ronnie, and Billy wheeled my gurney outside through the snow onto our patio and into our dining room. Finally, we were together again as a family around a single table, and I was thankful for these familiar surroundings and thankful that the long wait to sit upright again was nearly over. As Dad carved the turkey, I privately wished that he would also carve off my cast! But that ritual was still six weeks away.

Another aggravation during this period was a general lack of privacy. Since the age of five, I had grown accustomed to other individuals besides my parents assisting me in daily living necessities. When I became too heavy for Mom to lift, Dad would send over one of his assistants to dress me, drive me to and from school or to choir practice, or help me in going to the bathroom at school. Additionally, there was Helen, our housekeeper, who had been helping Mom in taking care of me since my third birthday.

These individuals met my needs and then would leave to fulfill their other responsibilities. When I needed them, they were there. When I didn't, they weren't. They added to my sense of autonomy from my parents and increased my confidence in being able to get along in life without constantly depending on Mom and Dad and my immediate family members to care for me.

We interacted for the sole purpose of them performing certain physical tasks that I was unable to perform for myself. They were not constant companions. There was a balance between depending upon others to help me and still being independent enough to feel as if I were not living life in a bubble surrounded by adult caregivers, not friends and family. They did not attend school with me, accompany me to sporting events with Billy and Dad, nor intrude upon the intimacy of our evening meals. All of this changed, however, when Ronnie arrived from Jamaica in January 1968 as my full-time caregiver.

When we met that summer of 1967 in Jamaica, Ronnie was available to help me when needed, basically, to aid Mom and Dad in lifting me in and out of the swimming pool or in and out of bed. But Ronnie had other tasks such as gardening and pool maintenance at the residence where we stayed in Montego Bay. Ronnie was not only blessed with a compact, powerful physique, but he also had an infectious laugh, boyish grin, and endearing personality. My entire family fell in love with him almost instantly.

When our tropical vacation was at an end, we didn't want to leave Ronnie behind. I asked Mom whether he could come to take care of me in Ohio, since my weight made it virtually impossible for her to continue taking care of me on those occasions when Dad needed his assistants at his office or the operating room. Mom said she would broach the subject with both Ronnie and Dad. Their response was favorable, but Ronnie's move to the United States did not happen overnight.

Mom said that Ronnie would need to meet certain immigration requirements before he would be permitted to enter the United States. I was under the mistaken impression that a simple plane ticket would do the trick. Mom and Dad would be required to demonstrate the unique skills that Ronnie possessed to be able to justify employing someone from another country. It took a full six months to process his application for a visa. In the intervening months, many letters were exchanged and questionnaires completed. Ultimately what made our wishes reality was the power and influence wielded by our Congressman, Wayne L. Hays. Famous for his arm-twisting and string pulling, Hays forced the Immigration and Naturalization Service to grant an exception in our case in light of my disability and issue Ronnie a twelve-month visa.

Once he arrived in Steubenville, I quickly realized that the relationship I had so much enjoyed while on vacation was an unrealistic honeymoon and did not manifest the personality conflict that surfaced. Ronnie was extremely helpful and enthusiastic for the first several months, but I still felt a lot of stress because of his constant presence. He expected to be included in practically every aspect of my life. Compounding this feeling of suffocation was a feeling of guilt because of all the time and effort that Mom and Dad had spent in bring him to America. So for the first several months, I said nothing. It was as if Ronnie were a new attachment to my wheelchair.

Following my spinal fusion and my return home from Rainbow, I was willing to overlook the stress that Ronnie's involvement in my life had created. It wasn't simply that he was always around, but the fact that Ronnie was extremely moody and his emotions could change abruptly. It wasn't long after my homecoming that Mom told me that she realized that Ronnie was causing a great deal of tension and she wanted to help alleviate it. She said that it was perfectly understandable that I felt the way I did towards Ronnie. Even the best of friends or the most loving of spouses get on each other's nerves if they are around each other too much, she explained. She suggested that she would assign Ronnie more household duties during those hours of the day when I did not need him. That helped to reduce some of the tension between us.

Modifying his job description, however, did nothing to improve his emotional stability. On some days he would be warm and engaging. On other days he would be distant and noncommunicative. I only escalated things by insisting that there had to be a reason for his reluctance to communicate. I was growing increasingly impatient about these dramatic mood swings. Invariably, things would culminate in heated arguments and mutual expressions of disgust.

Acknowledging the fact that Ronnie was indispensable to me from a physical standpoint, I resigned myself to continuing our relationship until such time that I could get along without him or at least find a realistic alternative. In short, I felt trapped by my circumstances. My physical needs at the moment outweighed my emotional happiness. Ronnie and I were fundamentally incompatible and this was my first relationship where I knew no matter what I did or tried things were just not going to work out. Ronnie never adjusted to Ohio's cold weather, and I never acclimated to his chilly disposition.

This continuing conflict, however, did nothing to deflate my excitement over the imminent removal of my body cast. Even Christmas 1968 could not compete with the sense of liberation and celebration that filled my mind and heart every time I considered what it would be like to sit in my wheelchair again and have the freedom to move about on my own. I could hardly contain myself when I thought of getting a complete haircut, feeding myself, and bidding farewell to bedpans! Of course, the sitting cast which I would have to wear for six months would have its own particular challenges, but I was sure that they would not begin to approach the trials that I faced while living a turtle's life for the previous six months.

On December 29, 1968, I was loaded into an ambulance to return to Cleveland and the fourth floor of Hanna House. On New Year's Eve, six months to the day of the operation, my plaster shell was taken off. Actually, it was sawed off!

I was amazed at how long it took. Cutting a cast the size and thickness of mine was no simple assignment. I had watched my father cut off many casts in his office, but they were usually on someone's wrist or ankle, not covering two-thirds of the person's body. I thought that the buzzing whine of metal biting into my cast would never end. Rather than feeling joy during this routine procedure, I was afraid that the resident's hands would slip and cut me instead of the cast. I guess I had watched too many Grade-B horror films! After thirty minutes the buzzing finally stopped and I, thankfully, was not bleeding. I had survived my prison!

When the cast was finally lifted off of me, I was struck by two simultaneous sensations. I felt both cold and weightless. I had not realized how the cast had had such an oven-like effect on my body temperature. It had retained more heat than I ever imagined and that explained why I couldn't stop shivering even though the nurses had placed a mountain of blankets on top of me.

But the feeling of weightlessness was even more shocking. My body felt so light that I thought I might float off the table if not for the weight of the blankets. For an instant, I even entertained the extraordinary thought that my legs might now be strong enough to stand on. That's how light I felt!

In addition to these feelings, there was another that I had not prepared for. I missed the cast! I felt so different and so disoriented without it. It had been my reference point for so long that it had become part of me. Now to be able to place my hands on my chest and stomach felt bizarre. I felt more pristine than naked. And to finally be able to have my thighs touch one another made me giggle with glee!

When I returned to my room and was lifted back into bed, Dad unwrapped a bottle of champagne that he had surreptitiously brought in under his raincoat. We cried and toasted and drank from small paper cups before having to confess our sins to a most forgiving nurse.

Mom could not believe how much I had grown in the last six months. "Let me look at you," she exclaimed. "You're a man! You're not my little boy any more!"

"But, Mom, I have all this dead, scaly skin all over me." I said.

"Oh, don't worry about that 'certza' (Serbian for 'dear to my heart'), I'll wash that off. Doesn't he look great, Bill?" she asked Dad.

Even the prospects of having to put the new cast on the next day could not douse her ecstasy. A hospital room never felt such warmth and never looked as bright as on that morning.

"For the first time in six months I feel like dancing," Mom declared. I not only felt like it, but in my weightless condition I felt like I could actually do it for the first time in my life. Then we toasted again to the new year and admired the straightness of my body.

Instead of watching bowl games the next day, it was back to the casting room to be fitted with a smaller, body-hugging, sitting-up cast. This new cast was half the size of the old one. It covered my shoulders, chest, stomach, and back. There was nothing behind my head and nothing covering my legs, which enabled me to sit up. But the pain and dizziness that I experienced prevented me from doing so for more than a minute or two over the course of the next several days.

Everything and everyone seemed out of proportion. My arms felt really heavy and everyone appeared so much shorter than they had for the previous six months when I was laying down. Swallowing was easier, but feeding myself was still impossible because of the need I had to lean forward and slump over my plate. I couldn't sit forward because of the cast, and so I wasn't nearly as independent as I thought I would be. Additionally, the cast, like my old corsets, would cut into my thighs. Needless to say, I wasn't happy with my new cast to the degree that I had dreamed. Mom said that things would improve after I got my stamina back, but I was disappointed and thought that the next six months would not be very different from the previous ones because I was so limited in what I could do.

After returning home in the first week in January, I resumed the seventh grade via my intercom system. Life was very much the same as it had been with the previous cast. I required help with practically everything, including eating. I felt so awkward in my new cast that I was unable to operate my motorized wheelchair, which was so critical to my independence. In short, things had not really improved. I was just living life from a different angle.

Chapter 10

We thought that I would be attending school some time in February, once I had regained my strength and could sit for a period longer than a couple of hours. But that never happened. Suddenly, in the middle of the night on January 23, 1969, I was awakened by a piercing pain. I could not catch my breath; I thought I was having a heart attack!

I had not felt particularly well the last couple of days. I had chills and felt somewhat nauseated. I thought I had the flu. I was sure of it.

The next morning, I felt worse. I began vomiting and was running an extremely high fever. Dad feared that I had pneumonia and an x-ray of my chest at the hospital confirmed his suspicions. My left lung was completely filled with fluid and I was sicker than I ever had been in my life. Immediately, I was admitted into St. John's Hospital in Steubenville and my physician, Dr. Jim Currant, prescribed intravenous fluids that contained antibiotics and nutrients. Dad called Drs. Herndon and Vignos in Cleveland to report my condition. He told them that the cast was restricting my breathing and asked if he could cut it in half to relieve my chest of needless pressure.

Loosening the cast would jeopardize the stability of the spine, according to Dr. Herndon. It was too early to take it off. The spine needed more time, but the pneumonia was not only jeopardizing my fusion, it was also threatening my life. Dr. Herndon said that he would have to supervise the cast's removal and monitor the spine. That could only be done in Cleveland. I was rushed there by ambulance.

It was a 125-mile drive to Cleveland and I felt every bump, curve, and stop along the way. I didn't think that I could take much more. I was breathing out of oxygen in my nose and vomiting continuously. There was only bile in my stomach by that time. I was really sick, but I didn't know how sick until I was taken to the intensive care unit. I knew things were serious because I was surrounded by physicians and nurses and very bright lights that they never turned off for the first couple of days.

Mom said that I was in critical condition because my left lung had collapsed and that is why I could not catch my breath. That is also why it hurt so badly to take a deep breath. Nevertheless I had to keep fighting. "Even though it's painful, honey, you can't stop trying to take deep breaths," she said. "Try to cough and spit out all of that junk in your left lung."

Then the real terror and torture began! My pulmonary specialist, Dr. Scott Inkley, was not at all confident that I would be able to discharge all of the thick congestion contained in my lungs. I could not do it by myself. I needed help. So nurses began suctioning my lungs every time I needed to cough or began to dry heave. Because I was so nauseated, they could not get the rubber tubing from the suction machine down my throat. They put vaseline on the end of the tubing and pushed it up through one of my nostrils down into my throat, which would not only gag me, but also cut off my airwave while they were suctioning. It was absolutely frightening! I hated every second of it.

They suctioned me every hour of every day and every night for a week. I could only sleep in an oxygen tank, which cut me off from the rest of the world. There was so much cool mist around me that I felt all alone, even when there were people present.

But Mom broke through the fog and the fear. Even when I could not see her face, she would poke her hand inside through the plastic tent to make a connection, to let me know that she was there. My hair was drenched with moisture, as were my face and neck, every time they would close me in my plastic bubble.

Still, my lung would not open! Doctor Inkley ordered respiratory therapy, which consisted of breathing into a machine that forced air into the lungs in order to expand them and break up the mucous that had invaded the remote areas of my chest. Then a respiratory therapist would begin a procedure known as "percussion." This procedure required the therapist to cup his or her hands and then rhythmically beat on certain selective parts of my chest, shoulders, back, and flank, as if playing a drum. The air caught between the person's body and the palms of the therapist created a hollow, popping sound.

The pounding and vibration caused a great deal of pain during these twenty-minute sessions. Once a particular section of the lungs was completed, the therapist then placed his or her hands on that area as I inhaled and exhaled deeply. During the exhaling, the therapist applied pressure to the area involved, which dislodged the mucous and made it easier to expel.

Percussion was not only painful and exhausting, it was also humiliating. Every time I would spit something into a tissue either a nurse or the therapist would have to assess its color and thickness.

Percussion was helping, but my lung remained collapsed. Dr. Inkley ordered another treatment — draining my chest of the fluid that he was sure was there. The procedure involved inserting a needle through my chest cavity and drawing it directly out from the infected area. A team of interns and nurses abruptly ushered my parents out of my room. They then unfastened the front of my cast, took it off, and sat me up in bed.

Next, the chief intern, Dr. Newsome, a man of unlimited arrogance with more of a graveside than bedside manner, began the procedure. I detested him but submitted to his callous instructions for the sole reason of getting better.

To have a long, thick needle inserted into a collapsed lung is an infinitely painful experience. But I was willing to endure it in order to reopen the lung and to extract the congestion that was restricting my breathing. Again and again, Newsome plunged, probed, and dragged the needle into my chest. I was crying and screaming in agony! Each time he would pull the needle out, I desperately asked, "Are you getting a lot of fluid?"

Dr. Newsome answered, "Not as much as I expected."

The nurses had brought two plastic buckets to hold the fluid that they were confident would be drawn out of me. After one hour, there was not enough fluid extracted to fill a tablespoon! Inkley's speculation and Newsome's incompetence combined to make this procedure a dismal failure and total waste of time.

Hearing my screams while standing outside of my room, Dad stormed through the door and shouted, "That's enough! Stop the procedure!" Newsome shouted back, "I'm the doctor! Get out of the room!"

The Third Opinion

Dad then said, "I don't give a shit who you are! You don't know what the hell you're doing! If you tap my son's chest one more time, I'll punch you in your God damn nose!" Dad continued, "Get Dr. Inkley on the line right now. I want to talk to him!"

But it was a Sunday, and Inkley was unavailable. Dad refused to accept that excuse.

When Inkley eventually telephoned, Dad was still fuming. He told Inkley, "I don't know what the hell kind of system you're running around here, but I will not tolerate some intern tapping my son's chest, when he doesn't know what the hell he's doing!" Dad then stated, "From now on, I want either you or another physician to perform any procedures on Stevie. I don't want another intern to come near him!"

Inkley listened and understood. Newsome was immediately taken off the case. We never saw him again. We jokingly referred to him thereafter as "Gruesome Newsome."

Dad had gained control and everyone, including Dr. Inkley, was now on the same page. Instantly, the entire staff became more attentive and courteous. It didn't hurt that Dad, for the first several days following the tapping procedure, was camped out beside my bed in order to stress his concern.

He was still the proud steel worker's son who spoke his mind without apology and without fear of offending anyone. Yes, my lung was still not open, but my spirits were lifted.

Dr. Inkley consulted with an ear, nose, and throat specialist named Dr. Maloney, whose expertise was in chest infections. Maloney was a welcome addition to the medical team. He was honest, competent, and, refreshingly, kind. I was thankful that he was involved.

That was before he described what he was going to do to me. At first it all sounded quite innocuous. He called it a bronchoscopy. What it entailed, however, was positively horrifying. Maloney said that he wanted to look inside my lungs to determine whether I had a tumor, pneumonia, or a pus buildup that had caused the lung to collapse. In order to accomplish that he would have to insert a hollow, stainless steel tube down my throat, through my trachea, and then inside both lungs.

He said that the procedure would be extremely uncomfortable, but then he promised that, from beginning to end, the procedure would take less than two minutes.

Maloney was right. The bronchoscopy was quick, but undoubtedly the longest two minutes of my life! First, my throat and tongue were anesthetized with assorted swabs and bitter tasting sprays. Before too long, it was difficult to speak and impossible to swallow. Second, my mouth was propped open with tongue-depressors and gauze pads until I thought my jaw would come unhinged. Third, my neck was bent back farther than ever before in order to create a straight line from my mouth to the chest. Then, Maloney walked in with his tool of torture. It was no tube; it was nothing more than a steel pipe. And it was at least three inches in diameter. It was so long and thick that I thought there was no way it would fit inside my mouth. The whole scene struck me as absurd.

Maloney had a determined look on his face. He told me to relax and close my eyes. He then began shoving the steel scope down my throat and into my chest. I wanted to scream for help, but I couldn't. I wanted to pull the pipe out from his hands but my arms were being held down by two nurses! All I could do was lie there, try to breathe, and cry. I was totally powerless and helpless!

I wanted to faint, but I couldn't! I prepared to die! I knew I was going to choke to death. Then miraculously, Maloney declared, "It's over! One minute and 45 seconds! You didn't believe me, did you? I kept my promise!"

I had just survived the most traumatic ordeal of my life. I was still grateful, however, that Dr. Maloney had kept his word and did not betray me.

He had good news. I *only* had pneumonia, not a tumor, and no pus build-up. Maloney said that he was able to suction as much as he could see while he was inside both lungs, particularly the left one.

When Mom was allowed to reenter my room, she wanted me to tell her every horrible detail. I was glad that she asked and that she cared. I told her how utterly violated I felt. I told her how sick I was of being sick. She said that it must have been awful, but that it was good news that Maloney had found only congestion and not a tumor. She said that things would now improve and that I had been through the worst of it. I was going to get better.

She was the only one who believed that. I wasn't sure of anything anymore. I thought I was going to lose my mind. Every time I thought I had endured the worst procedure of my life, it seemed as if the doctors would introduce another act of terror. I was running out of energy. And I was tired of fighting, hoping and praying. I was very close to giving up.

Mom wouldn't let me. She brought out her library of pep talks and sermons. I said, "Mom, I don't want to listen to those things any more. Don't read me any more Norman Vincent Peale sermons or stories about Jesus. They're not helping. I'm not getting better."

She said, "Okay, then you find something to read." She placed the Bible on my chest. She said, "Go ahead. If you feel like it or when you feel like it, just open it and begin reading."

What I did feel like doing was not reading, but just throwing-in-the-towel. Not only was I physically ill, I was spiritually sick, too. Neither the doctors nor the nurses could help me with my attitude. Just to prove Mom wrong, I opened the Bible for what I thought would be one last time.

I opened it to the Old Testament and began reading Psalm 86. It was called "David's Prayer." But I know that he wrote it with me in mind. He sounded tired and desperate, too. Someone else knew how I was feeling and had survived it. David captured my feelings with these poignant words:

> *Bow down thine ear, O Lord, hear me: for I am poor and needy.*
> *Preserve my soul; for I am holy: O thou my God, save thy servant that trusteth in thee.*
> *Be merciful unto me, O Lord: for I cry unto thee daily. Rejoice the soul of thy servant: for unto them, O Lord, do I lift up my soul....*
> *In the day of my trouble I will call upon thee: for thou wilt answer me. Among the gods there is none like unto thee, O Lord; neither are there any works like unto thy works....*
> *For thou art great, and doest wondrous things: thou art God alone.*
> *Teach me thy way, O Lord; I will walk in thy truth:*
> *unite my heart to feel thy name.*
> *I will praise thee, O Lord my God, with all my heart:*
> *and I will glorify thy name for evermore.*

David's prayer made me realize that I was not alone. He, too, had been at his wits end — so distraught. But, not forgotten or forsaken. During such hours and moments, God was not only there, but interested and involved. I learned from the Psalm that it is natural for us to turn away from God, throw our hands up in the air and sigh,

"What's the use?"

Although David felt so helpless, he did not run away from God. In his darkest hour, he asked God to help, knowing, intuitively, that help would come. I learned that during the coming days, I would need to lean on God's strength, energy and power. I could not survive and succeed without Him. I felt some how, some way, I would be rescued from this awful state. I could not give up on God because He had not given up on me. I was grateful that David had shared his inner turmoil. I made David's prayer my own.

My lung had not opened, but my spirit returned, more determined than ever to get well. Suctioning of my left lung continued hourly. The nurses assigned to me were not slightly empathetic. They never smiled, never engaged either Mom or me in conversation. They treated us like inanimate objects. Consequently, they provided me with an additional incentive to get out of intensive care. The suctioning, by comparison, was less annoying.

In fact, instead of having the nurses stick the tube up my nose, I volunteered to do it myself. Everyone was amazed that I preferred to do my own suctioning. I never liked it. I just disliked the nurses more.

But one night I got my revenge. I didn't plan it. It just happened. It was time for suctioning. My least favorite nurse was leaning over me as I choked and gagged on the tube that she had shoved down my throat. I needed to spit. I could have turned my head to miss her, but I didn't! It hit her squarely in her frowning face! I didn't offer an apology; she didn't deserve one. I never told Mom but I did share it with Snoopy.

Snoopy, my stuffed Peanuts' friend, played an important role in my hospitalization, beginning with my spinal fusion. He became indispensable during the long, chilly nights in the oxygen tent.

Mom, sensing my frustration, recruited Snoopy for a special assignment. He was my nighttime psychologist. Before leaving each evening, Mom would kiss me and say, "Now you try to keep warm, say a prayer and when you feel lonely or angry about being so sick, just tell Snoopy how you feel. He'll listen to you. He loves you."

She was right. Snoopy was a great listener. That was what I needed, just someone to share my frustrations and fears with. He offered no advice or analysis, just two floppy ears. He was always there when I needed him. Loyal. Peaceful. Quiet. Patient. Awake. He

The Third Opinion

never left my side and never has since those lonely nights in the oxygen tent.

He's very old now and in retirement. But he still lives with me and is there if I need him. He's not going anywhere. On occasions, I still awake him from one of his naps, just to tell him about my day or a problem that I am having. He's still a great listener and a tremendous friend.

After sixteen days I was finally taken off the critical list. My lung had opened and I was transferred to a regular hospital room. The suctioning stopped. The oxygen tent was no longer necessary. I was not going to die. I was thankful to be alive and breathing on my own.

Chapter 11

What was most exciting about my recovery from pneumonia was that for the first time since I was four years old I was thin again! During the two weeks in the intensive care unit, I had lost 40 pounds and trimmed 9 inches off my waistline. I weighed 105 and had a 27-inch waist. I couldn't wait to go shopping and say goodbye to my husky, monochromatic, wardrobe.

It was great to be thin. It was one less thing to worry about, especially with girls. I didn't mind that I was in a wheelchair. I did care that I was overweight, because I knew they cared.

Before leaving Hanna House and returning home, Mom offered me a retrospective of the battles that we had fought and the war we had won. She said, "You were so sick. But you made it through with God's help. You are stronger than you thought you were, even stronger, at times, than I thought you were. Now it's time for you to begin achieving your goals and becoming who you can become. You have a bright future ahead of you, honey.

"You will forget how sick you were, but I won't. These days in the hospital will fade from your memory, but not from mine. You will pass through other trials and tests and I will remind you of your story and these times when you hung on and survived. We've been through so much together and you're still so young that you won't recall these events and experiences. But I'll remember and I will remind you who you are and where you have come from."

Then it was my turn. "Mommy, I won't forget these times, and what we've gone through. You won't need to remind me." Then, my mind conjured those familiar images of FDR. He, too, had survived one physical trial after another. And he had come out of them stronger and more determined. I felt a surge of adrenaline pass through me. I realized, that I had been allowed to remain on Earth to help others and to restore their hope, like FDR. I didn't feel that I was being asked to carry a heavy burden or that these expectations that flowed from Mom's words were unrealistic or unreasonable. I wanted to handle it. I had shown that I could.

I liked the pressure of knowing that I had been given another chance to make a difference in people's lives. Every day counted and meant just as much as the last. I had to make the most of every day. I felt a certain degree of pressure, but in comparison to my nights in the oxygen tent and the horrors of suctioning, this was the kind of pressure that I didn't want to live without.

It had always been there, ever since Dad brought that magazine home. It was the pressure, the power and the passion of my life. I have never forgotten those two weeks in the winter of 1969. With that memory comes the humility and honor of being me.

My first official day of seventh grade didn't occur until the first week of April 1969, when I joined the rest of my McKinley classmates known as the 7-i's. Danny, Mary and Mike were there, along with David Teaff and Mike Turrentine and Karen Freeze.

Harding Junior High had six different groups of seventh graders. The top students of graduates from schools feeding into Harding comprised the 7-i's. The students with lower grade point averages and performance projections would be placed, respectively, into other classes. It bothered me that so many of my friends were being classified and labeled. These were kids who were feeling inadequate and mediocre. I knew I didn't like the stereotypes that surrounded my life in a wheelchair, and so I didn't like the stereotypes that many of my friends were now up against simply because their grades weren't as good as mine.

Besides this caste system, Harding Junior High had many different floors. Unlike the last four years at McKinley, I couldn't take my motorized wheelchair to school. I had to be pushed by a classmate in my manual wheelchair. None of my classes were held on the same floor. Science was on one floor, math on another, and social studies on still another. Consequently, I would have to be carried every day up and down narrow, steep stairways by my classmates. Mom said she couldn't think about having to entrust my safety several times a day to a band of thirteen year olds who would leap at the chance to help me in order to leave class two minutes early.

For the most part, I felt safe. Many times my brother Billy, an eighth grader, would leave his class early to navigate the back of the wheelchair, the most important part of the lifting. When Billy couldn't be there, Danny was. He was now well over 6'0" and closing in on 200 pounds! With either Billy or Danny behind me, to trust two other inexperienced carriers on each side of the chair wasn't that frightening.

What also helped in relieving the stress of transport was that I had the ability to explain in detail to others what they needed to do and how they needed to do it in order to help me. I was thankful that because Mom and Dad had recruited help in the past, and, in light of my hospitalizations, I had grown adept at articulating what my physical needs were and how best a person could help me in meeting them.

I not only enjoyed our time together on the stairs, but I also could feel that they appreciated that I was depending on them. I was simply their friend. That softened the bumpy rides up and down the stairs.

By the time school ended for the summer, I felt I was just hitting my stride. I was making good grades and was just as popular as I had been at McKinley.

But I did have a concern. I felt guilty that over the last year I had monopolized practically all of Mom's time and interest. Carole was off at prep school, so she didn't really need Mom's attention and feedback as much as Billy and Judy, who were still at home. Being in a hospital 125 miles from home made it impossible for Mom to be two places at once. She was so focused on our battle in the hospital that she talked of little else during her daily phone calls back home. She would ask all the usual questions, but it was obvious that she was preoccupied by my crisis-of-the-day.

Invariably, each conversation would turn away from what Billy or Judy were doing and settle directly on how I was feeling, hurting, worsening, or improving. Everything and everyone else in her world, of necessity and circumstance, became peripheral and I was responsible. I was the reason why Mom was absent from Billy and Judy's lives for that year. I didn't like it.

I knew both of my bookend siblings not only missed Mom, but were missing out. They needed Mom just as much as I did. They deserved her equal time and involvement. But my hospitalizations had changed that balance in their lives. My life had created a void in Billy and Judy's lives and there was nothing to fill it. Phone calls to simply report the events of the day were not enough for them or for Mom.

I was aware that my station in life, not position in the family, carried with it both positive and negative aspects. Mom and Dad often said that we were closer because of what we had endured and experienced by reason of my disability. Because of my relative immobility, we were acutely aware of each other's sensibilities and sensitivities. We talked to each other, played together. When we argued and fought we would quickly need to apologize and ask the other's forgiveness.

Mom and Dad's philosophy was that we are all in this together. But the "this" was "me," and I marveled how Carole, Billy, and Judy never complained, never resented me and never protested during times when my life took precedence over theirs. It wasn't because Mom or I wanted it that way, but because that was part of having a brother like me.

I tried to deflect as much attention away from me and redirect it onto them as possible. Without saying it, I wanted to compensate for which they were asked to do without — Mom's presence. Sometimes, I would deliberately lose a game I was playing with Billy, whether it was billiards, magnetic football or a board game just so Billy would feel good about himself. I never liked beating him at anything. I loved him too much to ever compete against him.

When my parents' friends would inquire about me while we were together at a restaurant, I would quickly respond in hopes that Billy or Judy would be given an opportunity to tell the audience what they were doing. Sometimes they were asked, but most of the time they weren't. That frustrated me. Why didn't people know them by name or ask them about school or how they were feeling? I never talked to anyone about it until much later in life. It still hurts that they went on without Mom simply because I needed her more.

Chapter 12

The summer of '69 was a glorious contrast to the previous summer spent worrying about and then living with my fused spine. I played at the swimming pool, flirted with girls, went on nightly drives with Carole, who had just gotten her license, and moved with the rest of the family into a new home.

Billy and I grieved over having to say goodbye to our ballpark/driveway on Braebarton, but throwing a whiffle ball was getting to be more work than fun for me anyway. The six months on my back had taken a serious toll on my pitching arm. Rehab and therapy couldn't return it to its glory days. So, it was just as well that we moved on. Besides, the new house on Lexington had other benefits with which the old house couldn't compete.

Unlike the old house, this new one was accessible. There were ramps to get me in and out. Once inside, there were extra-wide doorways that were wheelchair-friendly. When it was time to go upstairs, I didn't have to wait for Dad or one of his assistants to lift me. I merely had to open a closet on the ground floor and close the gate of my elevator! I could go to my own bedroom that had a built-in desk and waist-level light switches. Billy and I shared a bathroom that had an extra-high toilet seat, accessible sink and roll-in shower. My wallpaper was unabashedly patriotic — red and white stripes trimmed with a blue and white star-studded background. I told Mom that I felt like a dead president lying-in-state at the Rotunda!

What really topped it off, however, was that now we had our own indoor pool. I was becoming increasingly self-conscious at how children reacted to me at the swimming pool where I had spent so many of my summers. I didn't like them staring at me every time that Dad lifted me into and out of the pool. Plus, from a medical standpoint, Dad thought that the activity and circulation I could gain by swimming year-round justified the added expense. The pool was not only private; it also was equipped with a lift. I loved it because of the freedom and warmth that it provided.

Because of the elevator I could also reach the basement, whose main attraction was a pool table. We spent hours down there listening to our jukebox and playing pool. Since I was already at ball-level, my line-of-sight was quite clear and I soon mastered the game.

But my favorite part of the new house was definitely the backyard. Grass had nothing to do with it. The greatest portion was covered with an Astroturf six-hole putting green that allowed me to exploit my eye-to-hand proficiency.

I could putt either left-handed or right-handed, which meant that I leaned over either the right or left arm rest of the wheelchair and held the putter in what was then-considered an unconventional grip. I learned every crevice, wrinkle and seam of the carpet and the bruises on my chest from leaning over to make another putt were emblems of how much I enjoyed it.

Earlier that year, Dad purchased a Checker Cab that he drove to New York City to be modified so that I did not need to be lifted in and out of the car. I could simply stay in my wheelchair. The cab came with a free-swinging side door, a portable ramp, and a super-mini-wheelchair. Once being wheeled up the ramp, the wheelchair would take the place of a passenger seat. It would then be locked into place in wheel wells in the floor.

This cab was downright ugly. It was beige with a black top. It looked like a box on four wheels, and everyone saw us coming.

One afternoon, towards the end of August, Ronnie drove the cab to our community pool to transport us back home. I was not in the mini-chair; I was using my manual chair, which was larger and much more comfortable to sit in. When I traveled in this normal-sized wheelchair, I would be rolled up the ramp. From the back seat, Billy and Judy would hold the chair in place, since it could not fit into the wheel wells.

When we got home, we all got out of the cab. Billy and Judy ran into the garage. Ronnie was pushing the wheelchair towards the rear entryway when it suddenly sank into the grating that had been placed right in front of the garage. I felt tremendous pressure on both legs. An excruciating pain shot up my right thigh and I heard a snapping sound! I felt like I was going to throw up, not because of the shock, but because of the awful pain!

After I caught my breath I told Ronnie to run in the house. "Go get Dad, tell him I think I broke my leg."

When Dad came out, he felt my leg, and said, "I don't think you broke it, Stef, because you didn't fall out of the wheelchair. You probably either tore a muscle or sprained it."

"But, Dad," I said, "it hurts so much."

He said, "Let's put some heat on it, give you some Tylenol and get you in bed. I think you're going to be okay."

When Ronnie lifted me into bed, the pain again shot up my right thigh. I followed Dad's directions: medication, heat, relaxation. The pain persisted.

Mom and Dad said they had to meet another couple for dinner and that they would be gone for only an hour. Things did not improve. I vomited what little dinner I struggled to swallow, and the Tylenol and heat didn't slightly dent the pain.

When they returned from dinner, Dad was concerned. I could see it. He was puzzled, too. He felt my leg. Then he said, "Well, let's take you over to St. John's and x-ray it." I could tell, however, that he and Mom were skeptical. It made me angry that they weren't taking me seriously. I felt they questioned both my sincerity and the severity of my pain. I wasn't pretending; it really, really hurt.

Being lifted in and out of the car was agonizing. Mom was still impatient with me when I was placed on the x-ray table. Maybe she just didn't want to confront the reality that our lives were interrupted again by adversity.

The summer had been a recuperative time for her, too. Much of her life, particularly her relationship with Dad, had been postponed over the last year because of my health problems. She was thrilled with the new house. She was its primary architect. Most of the concepts and unique features of the home had originated with her. She deserved a rest.

When Dad entered the room with the x-ray, our summer ended. "You're right, Stef," he declared. "You cracked your right femur. See, you can see the line coming down the femur. Your muscles apparently are stronger than I thought."

The Third Opinion

I panicked. "Do you need to operate on it or put it back into place?"

"No, son," he said. "We have to put a long leg cast on it."

"Can I go to school?"

"Well, in a couple weeks, you can."

"Do I have to stay in the hospital?"

Dad said, "Well, just for a couple days until we stabilize the leg."

I didn't like any of his responses. They all meant one thing; more time in a hospital. It was a world that I hated. To be in a hospital only two miles from my home was particularly galling.

Mom, on the other had, was incredulous. She couldn't believe this was happening again. She also was apologetic. She was sorry that she had discounted my feelings.

I was still angry when they both left the hospital that night. There were no available rooms, so they placed me in a hallway bed. I hardly slept. But, Mom and Dad had gone. At least I was being cared for by people who believed my pain was real.

The next morning, Dad put a cast on my right leg that covered the area from my ankle to the top of my thigh. I was taken to a private room, familiar territory for both Mom and me. But what was so unfamiliar about this experience was that we were facing a different reason for being in the hospital. Unlike the hospitalizations for my spinal fusion and pneumonia, this visit was caused by a freak accident, a mishap.

My spine surgery was something we had elected to do and thus, to a certain degree, we had prepared and planned for. The pneumonia was an emergency, a matter of life and death. There was no time to prepare for it. It demanded our total commitment and focus. I was an innocent victim of infection and so it was easy for Mom to rally behind me.

This time was altogether different, though. We weren't confronting a major challenge — a spinal fusion. And we weren't fighting a ruthless enemy — pneumonia. We were inconvenienced by an accident, a minor aggravation when compared to what we had been asked to cope with in the last year. I wasn't going to die from a broken femur nor would the leg cast prevent me from attending the eighth grade. The only challenge appeared to be having to sit in my wheelchair with my right leg constantly elevated. No big deal.

That was at the heart of Mom's irritable mood. This hospitalization was totally avoidable. Ronnie only needed to tilt my chair on its back wheels to prevent the thin front tires of the wheelchair from sinking into the slots of the grate. But he didn't: It was understandable and excusable. None of us knew that my front tires were so dangerously narrow, that the grate would pose such a hazard to me. But they were and it did.

Mom and I were required to make sense out of this odd turn-of-events. I had to reassure her that we would meet this next challenge as we had the previous ones. I tried to sound and look upbeat. I downplayed the pain, just to show her how determined I was to adapt to my cast as soon as possible, so we could return home and resume our normal lives.

By the third day, things were looking up. I was being lifted out several times a day from my bed into a chair. I was able to feed myself and the only other thing left to learn was getting used to the awkwardness of the cast, especially in going to the bathroom.

But I was in a lot of pain. I tried not to think about it, but every time my right leg was moved, I could not conceal my grimaces nor control my choppy breathing. Dad had ordered Demerol for pain, and that helped for only about two-hour stretches.

Dad said that he had contacted Dr. Herndon in Cleveland about the accident and that he was relieved that I hadn't fallen out of the wheelchair. Still, Dr. Herndon thought that as a precautionary step my right hip joint should be x-rayed, just to ensure that it had not been traumatized in the accident.

I had not given my right hip a moment's thought since the hip-spica cast was taken off the previous December. I knew that Dr. Herndon was concerned that my curved spine was slowly pushing my hip joint out of its socket. With my new spine, I thought, the status of my right hip was no longer an issue. Consequently, when the technicians wheeled the portable x-ray machine into my room to take a look at my right hip, I was not even slightly concerned. Dad was at a neighboring hospital and would look at the film around noon.

I was just beginning my lunch when Dad walked in. I was sitting in a chair and feeling good about the progress I was making. I actually had an appetite.

Dad greeted me with his traditional "Hi" and then pushed his left hand immediately into my right hip. He asked, "Does that hurt?"

I answered, "No."

The Third Opinion

He did it again.

Identical response. "No, it doesn't hurt." I had a quizzical look on my face. "Why?"

Dad then said, "Son, your hip popped out of the socket. You dislocated your hip. I'm sorry. We have to go back to Cleveland to fix it. But we can't do anything until your femur heals a while longer."

I started screaming and crying. "No, no, I don't believe this!" I grabbed my tray of food and threw it off the table. Then I exclaimed, "I don't believe in God anymore. I'm going to become an atheist! God doesn't exist!"

I had never felt such rage before in my life. I was angry and bitter. And totally inconsolable.

Mom kept saying, "I'm sorry, I know how angry you are and how unfair this is."

I said, "No, Mom, you don't know how I feel! No one does!"

She corrected herself, "You're right. I don't know how you feel. I've never been through anything like this."

"Mom," I said, "this is a nightmare! I don't believe this is happening to me. It can't be happening!"

It wasn't a dream. Nor was it a nightmare. This was really happening. But I couldn't process it. It wasn't registering. I refused to accept the awful truth. I was in denial. And I just wanted to be left alone to brood, to sulk and to grieve the naive, faithful and trusting person I used to be.

I had already been through hell and back and there was no way I was going back to the hospital! I was subjected to enough torture in my lifetime! I had endured plenty of heartbreak and accepted my share of indignities!

I had fought the good fight. I had "taken-up the cross" on more than one occasion. I was well-acquainted with adversity, and I had learned all there was to learn about it. I knew what it felt like, hurt like, looked like, smelled like, and tasted like. I had plummeted its depths and courageously entered its recesses. Most importantly, I had survived.

But now, I was done. I wanted to get on with my life. I had been sick long enough. My life had been on hold for more than a year. It was time to be "me" again.

I wanted to go to school, play and watch sports with Billy. I wanted to talk on the telephone with my girlfriends, go out to dinner with my family, and go shopping for colorful clothes. A dislocated hip wasn't on my agenda.

Dad's news changed everything. It ruined my life.

Mom said, "You have every right to feel as you do. You should be angry. You should be mad. If you want to be angry at God, that's okay, too. There's nothing I can possibly say that will make you feel better or take away your anger. I think it's best if I leave you alone today, because obviously I'm just making things worse.

"I am so sorry that this has happened to you. If I could take this upon me I would, you know I would, but I can't. I know you don't feel like fighting anymore, and that's okay. But tomorrow, I'll be back and we are going to start over again. We are going to take one day at a time. And then, when you're ready we're going to continue the fight. It's too easy to give up. I've told you before, my love, every day is a new fight for us and this won't beat us either.

"So, tomorrow, I'm coming back and we will begin the fight again. Remember, God hasn't brought you this far to fail. I love you and I will see you bright and early tomorrow."

Mom recognized something that I did not. I was tackling adult issues and complex questions. As a child, I could not answer them. The news of the hip dislocation had changed me. By the time she returned the next morning, I was beginning to look at the world differently.

With her comments the previous day, Mom challenged me to meet her halfway. She cut some of the old strings that connected us and permitted me to find my own answers. She was never afraid of me losing my way. I am certain of that. I needed time to wander and wonder through this emotional wilderness.

When she returned. I was prepared to do battle and continue my development. I was still her son, but I ceased being a child. I was ready to grow up.

Chapter 13

The doctors in Cleveland concluded that since I would never walk, I really didn't need the head of my right femur. Consequently, rather than putting my hip back into place, they simply cut the head of the femur away. Other than some brief withdrawal from my dependence on Demerol as a painkiller, my recovery from hip surgery was smooth and brief.

My first day of eighth grade at Buchanan Junior High School occurred in November 1969. Because we had moved to our new home we could no longer attend Steubenville public schools, which was particularly disappointing. We were now part of the Wintersville (Ohio) School District, a smaller bedroom community to the west of Steubenville.

Aside from being very behind in mathematics, I was soon caught up in the other subjects. But the critical factor of the transition was that I was completely infatuated with another pair of Italian cousins — the Morrellis.

Marci was quietly seductive. She was sweet, considerate and humble about her great looks. No matter how many times that I would turn my head to admire her, she always smiled. Cheryl, Marci's cousin, was almost a polar opposite. She had a light complexion, blonde hair, and walked around school with "an attitude," twenty years before that term became an American colloquialism.

Cheryl knew how good looking she was; Marci did not. They were both cheerleaders and I looked forward to attending every home game. But besides the Morellis, I was also obsessed with Jeri Norris who was brazenly sexy at fourteen. I also was crazy about two

African-American classmates, Myra West and Linda Settles. Linda was an enigma to all of us. Painfully shy but exquisitely beautiful. I never broke through her defenses. Myra, on the other hand, was confident, outgoing and friendly. She was one of the first women in my life who could let me know that she knew how I felt about her without uttering a word. Wintersville wasn't such a bad place after all!

I fit into the "in" crowd quickly. I realized that I had certain skills that made my transition pretty successful. First, I was funny. I was open and candid about my disability and used my self-deprecating humor to reassure people that they didn't have to feel sorry for me or mistake me as someone who studied all the time.

Second, my teachers liked me. I answered a lot of questions and I performed exceptionally well on tests. I could tell that many of them were intrigued by my life and were secretly hoping for my success. Plus, they enjoyed my humor as well.

Third, everyone loved my unique way of laughing. Many people tried to mimic it, but with little success. They said it sounded like a seal barking at Sea World!

Finally, girls liked me because I could talk about anything they wanted to and I listened. I wasn't shy nor was I detached in hopes of being perceived as "cool."

I had evolved into the class "clown." I didn't need to listen in class all the time for fear of not comprehending the important parts of the lesson. Additionally, I loved all the attention I was getting from girls with my comic ability.

I needed to impress them during class time. I could not compete with my able-bodied friends after school on the basketball court or football field, when they were the center of attention. Thus, the classroom was not only a place for me to learn, but it was also the only place available for me to socialize and get to know females. The classroom was my domain.

By the time of my sophomore year, I was testing the limits of my teachers' patience. I had a quick wit and even quicker tongue. At times I crossed over the line from adding levity to a stuffy classroom to being a disruptive influence. One day, after receiving repeated warnings from my Spanish teacher, Mrs. Bloomfield, she asked a couple of boys to take me out of class. I knew that I was wrong and asked for her forgiveness the next day. But I hadn't learned my lesson.

The Third Opinion

Then the same thing happened in history class. The teacher was the varsity basketball coach, Dick Pannett. He wasn't a favorite teacher of mine nor was he popular at my house. Pannett was dogmatic, arrogant and rigid. He played only five players, practically all seniors, and never gave his younger, rising stars, like Billy, who was then a junior, a chance to play.

Billy was flashy and even a bit controversial. He allowed his hair to grow long. And he wore saggy grey basketball socks like his idol, "Pistol Pete" Maravich.

I knew talent and, laying all bias aside, Billy was a stellar performer who could have made a real contribution to the Wintersville basketball team. He had proven that a year before as a starter on the Junior Varsity Squad.

In one game, Billy's team had gotten shellacked by St. Clairsville in the first half. Billy had not played much or well. Then, in the second half he caught fire. He scored, passed and willed his team back from the dead. Still, Wintersville was one point down with ten seconds to go.

Billy took the ball from under his own basket. He dribbled past what seemed to be two or three inanimate objects. When he reached the foul line at the opposite end of the court, he fired his patented jump shot. The ball hit off the front of the rim and time expired.

But there was a whistle! Billy had been fouled! He got one last chance.

There were only two simple free throws that stood between him and a hero's immortality. He effortlessly approached the free throw line. After flawlessly bouncing the ball three times and rotating it fully once in his hands, he made the first. He tied the game.

Now, he could win it with the second. Again, he executed his ritual without a glitch. The ball swished through that net with the beauty and precision of the love and hope that had resided in my soul for this brother of all brothers! His teammates lifted him on their shoulders, but not as high as he deserved to be lifted. I couldn't stop shouting for joy. Mom and Dad were crying.

Finally, it was Billy's turn in the sun, his victory, his moment. I wanted him so much to feel it and revel in it. He deserved it, not only because he was a great player, but also because he was a great person.

Now as a member of the Varsity Basketball Squad, Billy was not playing at all. Game after game, I would sit with my parents and agonize about Billy's life on the bench.

Dad and I would admonish Pannett from the stands to send in the other players. Pannett would stand there stoically, totally oblivious to our criticism or the particular ebb and flow of a game. Consequently, my lack of respect for Coach Pannett carried over into the classroom.

It was embarrassingly obvious that Pannett was an equally underwhelming history teacher. My dislike for him was transparent and my classroom conduct was predictably unruly. I not only thought I could coach basketball better than he, but I also knew more about history.

When I wasn't verbally sparring with him, I was flirting with Karen Dailey. Pannett would glare at the two of us every ten minutes or so. Finally, he had enough. He directed some reluctant classmates to turn my wheelchair 180 degrees and push it into a corner. Then he instructed them to place erasers behind my back tires to prevent me from escaping. Everyone, including me, thought this was both ingenious and hilarious punishment, but ineffective in generating any respect for the coach-cum-history teacher.

Basketball was such an integral part of Billy's identity that his self-confidence waned during his season on the bench. His lack of playing time was affecting his concentration and study habits. Pannett was not going to change. It was clear that if Billy was going to play basketball, it would not be for this school and coach. Dad broached the subject of Billy going away.

My older sister, Carole, had begun attending an all-girls school in the ninth grade. Dad was never impressed with Steubenville public schools, particularly with the lack of financial commitment that was made by the community-at-large. It seemed as if each election year there would be another mill levy to support the schools that would be defeated by the voters. Before each vote, teachers would devote an entire class to lobby the students to support the proposal vis-a-vis their parents.

Also, Dad was concerned about the growing student/teacher ratios. Finally, he didn't like the number of basketball and football coaches teaching subjects other than physical education.

He always said, "One of the best gifts that a father can give his children is a good education." He was determined to do just that.

Carole attended the Greer School for Girls in Tyrone, Pennsylvania, near Penn State University, her freshman year in high school. Her

The Third Opinion

maturity level and sophistication had always been an irritant during her junior high school days at Harding. She grew impatient with the pettiness of the boys and the fickleness of the girls.

When Carole got to Greer, she blossomed. She was instantly accepted into a larger circle than she ever had in Steubenville. The other girls appreciated her strengths and were not threatened by her increasingly good looks. But Dad wasn't convinced that Greer was really a solid college preparatory school. He thought they spent too much time training the girls to horseback ride and not enough time teaching them how to study. It was more of a finishing school, so Carole stayed at Greer for only the ninth grade.

Dad found the type of school he was looking for in a posh suburb of Philadelphia, Bryn Mawr. Carole flourished at the Baldwin School for Girls, which was famous for its rigorous academic standards and well-heeled students. Carole definitely had found a place that would both challenge and nurture her.

Billy was in need of the same things. Dad, who clearly had a knack for this stuff, found a Pennsylvania prep school near the Maryland border, and soon Billy's esteem increased. The basketball team at Mercersburg Academy desperately needed a point guard of his caliber and Billy, at that juncture, just needed to be needed.

It was hard for me to let him go. We had always been together. I really missed him, but I was so relieved that he was now being appreciated for his talents. I was sad that I wouldn't be able to watch him play as often as I would have liked. But the strain in his voice was gone and so was the rejection from a misguided coach.

With Carole and Billy both away at school, I never seriously considered the possibility of leaving home to go to school as well. I envied them for the physical freedom that allowed them to live away from my parents' nest. Prep school sounded so romantic to me, too. I thought of ivy-covered buildings, spacious quadrangles, and boys attired in blue blazers, white button-down shirts and khaki slacks. But I knew that I needed to be practical. I would never be able to join these imaginary classmates on the quadrangle because of my disability. Prep school boys weren't strong enough or patient enough to replace Mom as my caregiver. Dad began exploring the possibilities nonetheless.

Pittsburgh, forty miles east of Steubenville, had a well-known boys prep school, Shadyside Academy. It just sounded exclusive. But Shadyside, like Baldwin and Mercersburg, was a boarding school. I would have to live there, so that wasn't an option. I was discouraged; Dad wasn't.

Dad remembered that two summers before, when Billy was attending summer school at Shadyside, someone had mentioned another prep school, north of Pittsburgh in Sewickley, Pennsylvania. The only thing Dad knew about Sewickley, up to that point, is that Sewickley was famous for being the home to many of Pittsburgh's industrialists. Most of Pittsburgh's top steel executives lived in Sewickley, since the town was upwind from the smoke stacks that dotted the valley.

After speaking to the Senior School's Headmaster, James Cavalier, Dad was impressed with Sewickley Academy. Unlike other prep schools in the area, Sewickley Academy was a country day school, not a boarding school. I would not be required to live in a dormitory.

Mr. Cavalier also said that the Senior School was on one level and completely accessible for a student in a wheelchair. More importantly, the school was academically demanding, with a strong faculty and small student/teacher ratio. The entire senior class had no more than sixty students. Finally, a Sewickley Academy education was comparable to any college preparatory education in the country, according to Cavalier.

The obstacles between a prep school experience and me were significant — where would we live and who would assist Mom in taking care of me? After touring the school, Mom did not believe there were any obstacles. All she kept saying was, "This is an ideal place for Stevie to go to school." So long as the school was accessible, she was determined to resolve the remaining issues.

Mr. Cavalier said that there was a very nice apartment complex one block from the Senior School. He believed that there was space available. Mom said, "Good, that's where we will live." Regarding the second dilemma, attendant care, Cavalier thought that if my parents contacted the D. T. Watson Home for Crippled Children, five minutes away, that perhaps a nurse or nurse's aide needing supplemental income may be just the kind of person we were looking for. Again, Mom said, "Great, that's where we will find some helpers. This is an ideal place."

Cavalier was amazed with Mom's confidence and desire to provide me with a prep school education. He believed that the academy environment was far from ideal for someone as disabled as I.

The Third Opinion

But after listening to Mom dismiss those concerns, he was convinced that she would make it ideal. Mr. Cavalier said that he would like to interview me.

Jim Cavalier was nothing like I anticipated and feared. He was not the stern headmaster that I thought always presided at such schools. He was warm, cheerful and very unassuming. He loved the Senior School, especially the students. As we toured the school, he knew all of the students by name and they greeted him with a "Hi, Mr. Cav!"

The students all seemed so bright and eager to learn. I felt that "Mr. Cav" wasn't intimidated by my disability, nor were the students. They smiled or said hello. They didn't stare and that made me feel that I could integrate more easily. Our Sewickley adventure was about to begin!

Chapter 14

Judy liked the Middle School as much as I liked the Senior School. One of the Academy's strengths, aside from academics, was its theater and dance program. Judy's interest in dance had grown exponentially over the last three years. Several times a week Mom would take her to Pittsburgh to be trained at Point Park College where she learned all types of dance, particularly ballet.

The Academy offered a dance program that was diverse and performance-oriented. Its dance director was the popular choreographer Mario Melodia, known for his flamboyant personality and singular ability to transform a group of stiff, reticent preppies into a show-stopping chorus line. Mom and Judy were thrilled. Now our dancer would dance every day.

Although I was sixteen years old, I had not gained much weight since my two-week stint in intensive care three years before. That made taking care of me much easier and expanded our options. Mom found two female nurses to share the morning and evening duties. They were both ideal for their very distinct jobs.

Vi Marion was my morning nurse. She worked graveyard and so would leave the hospital at 7:00 a.m. each weekday morning and arrive at my apartment at 7:15. She was shy, fast and efficient. She would :lift me into a shower chair, shampoo my hair and wash me in about ten minutes. Then, she would lift me into our walk-in closet that we converted into a dressing room. The distance between the bathroom and bedroom was too far and so Mom purchased a dressing table that had a cushioned surface that enabled Mrs. Marion to dress me there, rather than on my bed.

The Third Opinion

Everything about my relationship with Mrs. Marion was a routine, but a routine that brought predictability and love during my two years at the Academy. We never deviated from our morning regimen. I would ask her about the weather, what kind of night she had had in the hospital, how much sleep she had gotten during daylight hours, what she had eaten for dinner the previous night, whether she was able to catch a brief nap at work and what she had planned for that day once she slept four or five hours. Her energy level amazed me. She yawned three times in the two years that she helped me! The only time that she would depart from her morning routine was to tickle Judy as Judy was stretching her legs on the bathroom sink. Mrs. Marion's giggles were a brief reminder that she was able to have fun, but we simply had too many things to do before we needed to leave for school.

Once in my wheelchair, I would eat from a breakfast menu of my own devising. I never enjoyed breakfast food. Cereals, eggs, and pancakes struck me as either too juvenile, too bland, or too messy. Juices were just as unimaginative. Mom insisted that I eat something. Years before she had relented and allowed me to substitute tomato soup, cottage cheese and crackers with either tomato juice and hot chocolate. Mrs. Marion would then help Mom or Judy lift me in the car.

These morning lifts by a diminutive nurse, and a petite, but powerful, fourteen year old sister were works-of-art. Mrs. Marion would get behind me and clasp her hands on my chest with both arms underneath my arm pits. Since my head would fall backwards if unsupported, Mrs. Marion would hold me tightly against her chest. I would make two fists and place them both against my face to prevent my arms from floating upward during the lift.

Judy was responsible for the bottom half of my body. She would place her left arm underneath my knees and her right hand would be positioned under my calves. Judy, so agile and strong, would gingerly guide my legs into the car without banging my overly sensitive ankles and feet, while Mrs. Marion would slide the top part of me in as I pressed my fists into my cheeks to maintain a cradle under my arms. Sometimes, for comic relief, Judy would imitate how distorted my face was during these lifts, which only served to unify us more as a great morning team.

My night helper, Adele O'Connor, shared very little in common with Mrs. Marion. She was much larger, single, man-crazy, a gossip and a nonstop talker. Her written job duties were to undress me, place me on the toilet and put me into bed. It only took her a half hour. But in that half hour, I delighted in playing her straight man. She was a nightly comedienne. If Rush Limbaugh had a great aunt, this lady was it!

I would merely lead her into one of her favorite subjects: men, Mrs. Marion, minorities, Richard Nixon, Watergate, and even my parents, and she would pontificate and hyperbolize about everything and everyone.

Mom would chide me for goading Mrs. O'Conner into her nightly harangue, but I only did it to entertain us both during a rather boring ritual. I said, "Mom. Look, I'm seventeen years old; she's forty-seven. She's here basically to help me go to the bathroom every night and wipe me when I'm done. We've got to talk about something. Mrs. O'Conner loves talking about herself and her world. She's lonely, obviously. I listen to her and enjoy her. She breaks the monotony and leaves me every night with a smile on my face. I think she needs me as much as we need her. She's a character. Don't worry, I don't take her opinions and prejudices seriously, even if she does.

By far, the individual most valuable, and most critical in meeting my physical needs was Judy. Judy was the person whose help I relied upon most often during the two years that I attended the Academy. I weighed approximately 110 pounds; Judy, 100.

Nevertheless, she was able to lift me in and out of my wheelchair, if no one else was around to help. Among my siblings, I preferred Judy to help me. She was not only blessed with an athletic, durable body, but also she understood mine better than anyone in my immediate family, with the exception of Mom. She had the strength but just as importantly Judy had the sensitivity and compassion to know how to take care of me. Her touch was tender and her heart was always willing.

Since our apartment only had two bedrooms, Judy and I were roommates. As a matter of convenience, Judy replaced Mom as the primary turner at night. That was something that needed to be done two or three times a night and had been since I was a baby. Judy, did it better than anyone, including Mom.

Most nights I would begin sleeping on either my left or right side. A pillow would be wedged behind my back and another between my legs. After a couple of hours sleep I would wake up because of an

The Third Opinion

aching shoulder or cramped leg or other part of my body that was either asleep or causing pain or pressure. Consequently, I would need to be turned to my opposite side or placed on my stomach.

When I was in pain or discomfort, I would call Mom or Judy to turn me. Some nights I would turn once, if I were really tired. I would turn three times before morning. On restless nights, when I didn't sleep well because of school or romantic worries, I needed someone else to "toss and turn" me.

Before we arrived in Sewickley, Mom was chiefly responsible for my nightly turns. She would get up every time I called. Turn-after-turn, night-after-night, year-after-year — for fifteen years! At times, Dad would get up, or if Billy heard me before Mom, he would turn me. For the most part, turning was Mom's job.

No matter how habitual the turning procedure got, there are too many fine points to enable a person to do it "in their sleep." Mom only had uninterrupted nights when she and Dad vacationed — no more than three weeks a year. That is a lot of turns and a lot of partially wakeful nights.

Turning me from side-to-side at night was another aspect of my life that had to be done. It was done expertly and lovingly by a selfless mother and a caring kid-sister in the darkness, when nobody else knew and nobody cared, except me.

In addition to the turning, Judy also assumed other duties. She not only helped Mrs. Marion lift me into the car every morning, she assisted Mom in getting me out of bed in the evening following my nap and even volunteered to take care of me on the toilet, if she were closer than Mom.

Just as important, she provided much needed companionship. Except for nights when she was taking another lesson or rehearsing for one of the many musicals or plays she was in over these two years, Judy spent her evenings at the apartment studying, watching television and listening to my reports on my latest crush. On weekends, when we left Sewickley and traveled home to Steubenville, Judy would willingly stay with me rather than elect to spend time with a classmate. With Judy as my roommate at school, I was confident and secure because she took care of so many of my physical concerns and social needs. I credit her for the success I enjoyed at the Academy.

From the very start, I was intellectually challenged and stimulated by the curriculum. It was positively exciting that there were so many elective courses to choose from. My very first class was in Russian History, with only eight total students enrolled. I took Situational Ethics, 20th Century America, and a host of other courses that struck me as terribly collegiate.

Assignments were meaningful and demanding. The majority of instructors were young and enthused about their subject matter. The whole place was infused with such a dynamism that I looked forward to learning, asking questions and studying.

I wasn't alone. Many of my friends at the Academy were outstanding students. I was popular among my classmates and even had a nickname, "Steuby," referring to the fact that I was from Steubenville. They enjoyed my sense of humor and I was touched by how much they cared about me. Many of them, such as Peter Stinson, Howison Schroeder, Brian Buckley and Ted Waller, were always eager to help get me out of the car in the mornings or help me get books out of my locker. These boys came from extremely affluent families. They were accustomed to country clubs, chauffeurs and maids. They were used to being served. Now they were serving and sacrificing their time and muscles for me.

With few exceptions, like Hal Partenheimer, the athletic director's son, and Tim Appleton, a prolific basketball scorer (he was the top scorer in the State of Pennsylvania 1972–73, with an average of 44 points/game), these new friends were not jocks. They played sports such as soccer, basketball and the Academy's most popular game, lacrosse, but they were not natural athletes. In that sense, they differed from my public high school friends. They were more reminiscent of the Kennedys whose love of sports was rooted more in family and social tradition.

One day, during our morning announcements, when the entire Senior School would gather in the library to listen to Mr. Cav present us with a quote or philosophical thought that was followed by a calendar of upcoming events, Mr. Cav declared: "Remember, gang, spectator sports will never solve the major problems of the world." I remember that tingles went down my spine. I felt so energized by that statement. I felt empowered and vindicated, too.

Sports, in my life, had always been entertainment or a means to bond with Billy or my friends. So many around me had elevated athletics to such importance that I had always felt somewhat inferior to other boys. Athletics as a form of self-expression were gradually

The Third Opinion

being closed off to me altogether as result of my weakening hand and arm muscles. That one sentence had evened the score, placed me on the same footing as everyone else, maybe even tipped the balance in my favor. It crystallized my educational experience and lifelong ambition to make a difference in people's lives outside the realm of sports.

I studied long and worked hard for the great grades that I got. I would never be a famous athlete. But that really didn't matter; ideas mattered, according to Mr. Cav. They were what finally resolved conflicts and addressed society's problems such as poverty, violence, war, disease, racial and ethnic injustice and inequity. Mr. Cav's axiom was nothing more than a reiteration and reaffirmation of what Dad told me when I was four years old. I had a gift — my mind — I needed to develop it and expand it to help others. That's what life was about.

Now, in a single sentence, Mr. Cav had captured my entire life and the vision that had propelled me through challenge and loneliness. I had always been on the right track. Mom and Dad had given me a head start. I was excited to be me. I left that assembly with tears in my eyes and a lump in my throat. I felt just as strong and just as valuable as any athlete in my school or in the world that day.

The girls in prep school were different, too. Unlike many of my friends and loves in public schools, these girls appeared oblivious to most of the guys and even less concerned about their appearances. In short, they didn't care how they looked or how they dressed. They never wore make-up, high heels, painted fingernails, or nylons. Their wardrobes consisted of jeans, painter's pants, clogs, oxford button-down shirts and argyle sweaters.

When they wore a skirt, it was not only a major event, but also a kilt with knee socks. Few, if any, bothered to shave their legs. Curling their hair was out of the question. Many of them were bold and brash. They had definite opinions. And they weren't shy about sharing them. They were not intimidated when boys disagreed with them. I liked that about them, but their unfeminine appearance was cause for concern. I really missed my "public" girl friends for several weeks.

I searched for someone, anyone in this haven of disinterested females who was attractive. I thought "sexy" and "pretty" were on the endangered adjective list, but then I discovered a wonderful exception.

I saw her at morning announcements. She came into the library, after Mr. Cav began. No one seemed to notice her, except me. She was the quintessential preppie. She was wearing a blue oxford, white painter's pants and Dr. Scholl's sandals. She had dark brown hair that already had strands of grey through it. Mascara was her only make-up. That was perfect. She didn't need any accentuation.

Suddenly, there weren't enough words in my vocabulary to describe her. I immediately looked for "Teddo" Waller. He had basically been my tour guide for the first several weeks. He fancied himself a real ladies' man but he had not mentioned anything about this revelation of womanhood! "Teddo," I said, "Who was that girl who walked into morning announcements late and was with Andy Stone and Peter Stinson?"

Teddo said, almost derisively, "Oh, that's Laurie Stinson, Peter's sister."

"Is she his older or younger sister," I asked, hoping she was only a sophomore.

Teddo again matter of factly stated: "She's a senior."

"Does she have a boyfriend," I asked, already dreading an affirmative response.

"She did last year, but he graduated."

"Is she dating Andy Stone?"

"No, I don't think so; I think they're just friends and they just hang out a lot together."

I couldn't believe it. This was too much to ask. No boyfriend, no one that Teddo was interested in pursuing, and an older woman. Although Laurie was a senior, she wouldn't graduate until June 1973; I had nine months.

It was a great beginning. Peter Stinson was already a friend. I learned that Laurie was a dancer, so Judy would probably know of her and, perhaps, even be in a dance class with her. Plus, Laurie was in choir, our only class together. But when I saw her in the halls or at choir it seemed like I couldn't make eye contact long enough for us to exchange a "hello." And she would have to say it first. That was always a rule with me. I never said "hi" to anyone first. I was afraid of rejection. That created a problem. Laurie wasn't "stuck-up," only shy. I couldn't conceive of anyone that beautiful and bright being shy. At least, she wasn't boy crazy. Eventually we met. Peter introduced us one day. With that accomplished, I could handle the rest. With Laurie

The Third Opinion

as my love interest, my transition into prep school was complete and my transformation as a preppie had begun.

Mom and Dad were more than amused that my new love was Laurie Stinson. Laurie and Peter's father was Chairman of the Board of National Steel, in Pittsburgh, parent company of Weirton Steel, the company that had employed my paternal grandfather, John, for forty years and that had blackballed my maternal grandfather, Stephen, after he had asked for a 50 cent a week raise.

I was too busy assimilating into preppie culture to ponder the irony of my friendship with Peter and Laurie Stinson. I was learning how to dress differently and even talk differently. Not until I got to the Academy did I realize that I had a "Pittsburgh" accent. According to my new friends, that was a real disability, more noticeable than being in a wheelchair.

To rid myself of "Pittsburghese," I had to learn what I was saying that was so improper. Assorted friends pointed out some of the telltale signs by exaggerating the pronunciation of words such as downtown (dabntahn), doing (dewin), you (yunz), steel (still), no (nah) and get out (git aht). Of course, my accent wasn't that egregious, but it was evident that I needed some help. Before long I reformed my language and was considered a recovering "Picksburgher."

I was also introduced to "preppified" rock music. One of my new Academy friends was a soft-spoken, perma-grinning hippie named Matt MacWilliams who constantly condemned my musical preferences for groups such as Deep Purple, Humble Pie and Grand Funk Railroad. Matt and his sidekick, Duncan Wilcox, tried to recruit me as a disciple of the Steve Miller Band, the Allman Brothers Band, Roy Buchanan and the Academy's rock "god," Jesse Colin Young, who resembled an emaciated David Crosby. In fact, in the Class Yearbook that featured favorite quotes from the Seniors, Mr. Young easily outdistanced every poet, philosopher, and religious leader as the most quotable celebrity. Even when I pledged my allegiance to such emerging icons as James Taylor and Crosby, Stills, Nash and Young, Matt was not convinced that I had purged myself of my heavy metal rock roots.

In comparison to my musical tastes, my musical talents were better appreciated at the Academy. I looked forward twice a week to being able to leave the Senior School campus and travel down the road to the newly-constructed Fine Arts Building where choir practice was held. Because the Fine Arts Building was multi-leveled, with no elevator, I would need to be lifted up several steps to enter at the bottom level of the building where the large rehearsal room was located.

It was such a novelty to attend choir while at school. I couldn't believe that I was receiving a grade and earning credit for something that I loved so much. I had attempted to play musical instruments as a child, but the instruments themselves were always too heavy and therefore too physically demanding. I explored the piano, guitar, and melodica (that requires the player to blow into it while playing a keyboard). I could not read music and even though I took lessons for all three instruments, it was obvious to me that there was no sense in investing more time or money in any of them.

On the other hand, my voice was something that I could totally control. From my days in St. Paul's Choir, I took pride in knowing how to breathe properly and end a song on beat. My voice was the only instrument left that didn't require arm or hand strength.

Another attraction was that the Choir Director, Carol Duffus, was quite pretty. To have both Laurie and Mrs. Duffus in the same room twice a week was heavenly. What really fueled my fantasy about Mrs. Duffus was the rumor that while she was in college, she had been a Playboy Bunny!

For the Christmas program at the end of the first semester, Mrs. Duffus asked me to sing a solo from the Negro Spiritual "Go Tell It On The Mountain." The next semester I was featured in another song with two other classmates during the choir's performance of "Godspell." I was angry that I had to share center stage with two other guys. I felt that I had one of the better voices in the choir and that Mrs. Duffus was elevating others above me, but I would get my revenge later that spring.

Chapter 15

We took "Godspell" on-the-road to Toronto, Ontario. Anticipating the trip was much more thrilling than the actual experience, however. Instead of going on the bus with the rest of the choir, I had to fly to Toronto with Mom and Dad. We stayed in a hotel in downtown Toronto, while my classmates were assigned families to stay with in the small town of Scarborough where we performed.

Scarborough's High School was depressing and disappointing. I thought that we were going to be performing at another prep school that resembled the Academy. The high school was not a college prep school, but was more of a trade school that trained students in technical, automotive, and electrical skills. Even more disappointing was that the school was populated by tough, street-wise kids who appeared much too cynical to be an appreciative audience. They reminded me of the type of students that Sidney Poitier confronted in "To Sir With Love."

Our two performances were sparsely attended and, although the audiences were attentive, the gap between our cultures was still evident by the time we departed. The only redeeming part of the trip was that we were required to learn the Canadian national anthem "Oh, Canada." I concluded that life on the road as a "rock star" had its negative aspects.

The most intriguing part of Sewickley Academy's curriculum was the "May Program." The faculty believed that Academy students were under great pressure to compete and excel. Grades and class rank were taking precedence over learning. Consequently, many students would shy away from taking certain classes in fear of lowering their G.P.A.'s. The May Program was designed to allow students to choose an array of diverse subjects, free from the stress of grades. All the courses were pass/fail.

I learned that the dance and theater director, Mario Melodia, was offering a mini-course entitled "The Best of Broadway." I believed that the class would require nothing more than reading a number of popular plays from the Broadway stage, with a free-wheeling analysis of plots, characters and production. I was sadly misinformed. I should have known Mario Melodia would never do something so sedentary.

Mario was first and foremost a performer. Not surprisingly therefore, the "Best of Broadway" was an intense, month-long, amateur Broadway musical production including selections from *Cabaret, Oklahoma*, and *West Side Story*.

Mario only wanted people who were active, energetic and dedicated. I believed I satisfied these prerequisites. He also required that everyone act, sing, and dance. I was discouraged. Mom said that my life-long desire to perform on stage was at least worth a talk with Mario. Mom said surely there had been some play or musical that had included a role for someone in a wheelchair. She couldn't think of one, however. I assumed that such a character would probably not be found in a musical because dancing was an integral part of every musical. Still, Mom said, it was worth a try.

Two weeks before the May Program was to begin, I telephoned Mario and made an appointment to meet with him. At the meeting, I could tell that he was intrigued about the possibility of including me in the course. He said that he needed a couple of days to search his memory of musicals. That's all he needed.

A couple of days later, Mario said he had found a musical and one of the leading roles involved a character in a wheelchair. It was not an obscure musical. It was Neil Simon's "Little Me." Sid Caesar, in 1962, originated the role of the elderly miser named "Amos Pinchley" who used a wheelchair and whose life changed for the better when a beautiful young woman from the other side of the tracks broke through his barriers of bitterness and greed. Mario said that he had already begun choreographing a number around my wheelchair. He was excited and I was thrilled!

Mom was ecstatic. She said, "I'm proud of you for having the courage to tell Mario what you wanted to do. Just because you are in a wheelchair doesn't mean you have to miss experiences that other teenagers are enjoying. You're talented, too. You can act and sing. This will be really no different than singing a solo in the choir at church or at school." She then said, "I'm sure that the performance of "Little Me" will be the best of "The Best of Broadway." Then, we exchanged our patented "High-Fives" as Mom leaped in the air.

As Amos Pinchley, I needed to tap my full range of emotions. Initially, Amos was gruff and detached. Once the female lead, Belle Poitrine enters the picture, his icy disposition melts. Amos becomes a real person. Ultimately, Amos and Belle celebrate his transformation by singing and dancing with a twenty-member ensemble. Donna Kaufman was my co-star and guided my wheelchair with rhythm and skill.

I was dressed in a gray suit, vest and high-collared shirt. The best part was definitely my make-up and hair. Lines were drawn on my face and chin to make it appear aged and wrinkled. Then, a mustache and bushy eyebrows were added. My hair was curled and teased in Einstein-like disarray and then sprayed with white highlights. The result was an octogenarian who appeared as someone who ended up in a wheelchair due to the march of time, not because of a congenital muscle disease. My costume compensated for all my boyhood Halloweens when I could not disguise my wheelchair.

I loved everything about this experience: the countless rehearsals, the staging, learning my lines and the panic of opening night. We had a limited run of only two nights. But I had done it! It was a great achievement!

I felt like a pioneer. I was making a statement about my value and talents. My two nights on Broadway meant more than being the first full-time student in a wheelchair in the history of the Senior School.

I was sure that there were other prep students in wheelchairs, who had distinguished themselves academically. But by performing on stage, I had shown the audience and my classmates that I had more to offer than my intellect. I had other gifts besides my brain that needed a forum for expression. There was more to me that just someone who knew how to study and get good grades. I had shown everyone that I was more versatile than their stereotypes of what persons with disabilities could do. I wanted them to see me as I saw myself; as someone who had so much to give and offer the world in spite of the fact that I couldn't walk.

The crowd was entertained and educated. When it was my turn to take a bow, I took it proudly for Mom and Dad and me. I could hear their applause above the rest of the crowd.

I took "Yoga" as a second mini-course, not to fulfill a dream, but because of my lust for the instructor, Mrs. Julie Korpi — "the Latin from Manhattan," as we called her. While she taught us proper breathing and meditation, I was preoccupied how great she looked in her leotard and fish-net stockings. My heart beat increased and I actually believe that I perspired during a couple of classes!

In addition to this brief career as a thespian and Yogi, there were two other events that demonstrated my desire to be accepted and understood by my peers. The first occurred two months into my junior year at the Academy. Since the Checker Cab was too small to transport my motorized wheelchair, we left another motorized chair at school over night to be charged so that the two batteries would not be drained for the next morning. We kept the chair in the custodian's room, which was a popular loitering area for some students who stopped by to talk to the custodian, Alex Berry.

One morning when we arrived at school, a student reported to us that it looked like someone had been riding around in my wheelchair. It was completely drained of power. It was unplugged from the charger, and its footrests were askew.

Since Alex's room had no chairs, except one for him, I assumed that my wheelchair would be used by students to flop into during their "rapping-with-Alex-sessions." We made signs for the students instructing them not to sit in it.

Ever since I was a child, and got my first motorized wheelchair when I was eight, I never liked anyone sitting in it. To me, the wheelchair is more than a means of transport to get me from one place to another, like a car or bicycle. It is part of me. It is integral to my identity. For an able-bodied person to treat it as if it were just any ordinary chair, diminishes its value and importance.

What further annoyed me was when a person wants to drive the chair. To me that is insulting for anyone to treat it as some kind of battery-operated toy. The wheelchair is not entertainment; it is my life. Unlike my able-bodied friends, I cannot ride in it for a couple of minutes and then get out of it. It functions as my legs. I can't move without it.

That morning it was obvious someone had not only sat in my

chair, but had also taken it on a joy ride. I couldn't use it for the entire day.

Before morning announcements, Mom and I went into Mr. Cav's office. We explained what happened. Mr. Cav was very upset. He said, "Well, we will get to the bottom of this, right now. I'll talk to the students and tell them not to go near your chair."

I interrupted him. "If it's okay with you, Mr. Cav, I would prefer to talk to the students myself. It's my chair, after all."

At the end of announcements, he said, "Now, Steve Mikita, would like to take a few moments to talk to you about an issue." I didn't have much time to gather my thoughts. I knew that I had to get my point across without offending anyone and without leaving the impression that I was overreacting. I needed to express my concern without being emotional. This was a teaching moment.

"Thank you, Mr. Cav. Something happened this morning with my electric wheelchair. When we got here, my chair wasn't working. Apparently, last night someone took it out for a joy ride. It needs to charge for eight hours for me to use it the next day.

"Now, I know that an electric wheelchair is a novelty. Everyone is curious about how it runs and how fast it goes. But a wheelchair is not a toy. It's something that I feel is part of my body. I really depend on it and if it isn't working, then I have to be pushed from class to class. That really restricts my independence. So if you would not sit in it or ride in it, I would appreciate it. And I'll make you a promise. If you don't mess with my wheelchair, I won't walk in your shoes!"

Everyone howled. My remarks were successful. I had made my points without separating me from them. I was happy that Mr. Cav had permitted me to handle my problem in my way. I believed that if he had done my talking for me, I might have been misperceived as weak or a whiner. By addressing the student body myself, I disclosed a part of who I was, a very personal and private part. I taught them my approach to my wheelchair.

Many of my friends said they loved my remarks and wondered aloud, "Who the hell messed with your chair?" I never found out who the culprit was, but no one ever took it for a spin again.

The second incident occurred in September 1973, during my senior year. The seniors congregated in the largest classroom, which was multi-tiered. I was sitting at my familiar perch in the back of the room. The purpose of the meeting was the election of class officers. I secretly hoped that someone would place my name in nomination, but I knew that was really pretty unrealistic, in light of the long-term relationships and well-established cliques that preceded my admission into the Academy.

Mr. Cav solicited nominations from the floor. Howison Schroeder raised his hand and said, "I nominate Steve Mikita for Senior Class President." I couldn't believe it! Howison was a good friend, but not someone who I expected would do something like this. He was so much closer to other guys in the class. Other names were proposed — Doug Birmingham, Tommy Gordon, Stephanie Erb. I thought that Tommy was the clear front-runner. He was extremely popular.

After all the nominations were proposed, Mr. Cav instructed the presidential nominees to put their heads on their desks while a silent poll of hands-in-the-air was conducted. One by one our names were presented to the voters. When the voting ended, Mr. Cav said we could open our eyes. When I opened mine, I saw that everyone's eyes were riveted on me. I had just been elected President of the Senior Class by an overwhelming majority! Everyone broke out in spontaneous applause and I broke out in tears. I was speechless.

It was a breathtaking achievement. It signified more than mere acceptance and integration into my class. For me, the election recognized my ability to appeal to diverse audiences, to cut through the typical coalitions and conspiracies that pervade any high school. My classmates gave me their confidence and designated me their leader, their spokesperson, their servant. I was jubilant as were Mom and Dad. I thought about FDR that day, too.

Mr. Cav never called me "Steve-o" after that day; I was "El Presidente."

As Senior Class President, I desired to do something unique or extraordinary in order to leave my mark on my class and the entire school. I began soliciting suggestions from my classmates. My platform was simple. No one could remember the last time the Senior School had held a prom. I was incredulous. In public high schools, proms were indigenous to the culture. How could you say you went through high school without going to a prom?

That is what I would give my socially deprived classmates — a prom. Not surprisingly, there were quite a few friends who believed that proms were obsolete. Proms were what public students did, not preppies.

The Third Opinion

But I forged ahead anyway. I had a good enough understanding of politics to realize that I couldn't listen to every constituent. Plus, I disarmed some of the prom's harshest critics by recruiting them for a host of the subcommittees that I formed to decide on the music, menu, and venue. All that remained was both a private and public decision — who would I invite as my date? It was one of the toughest decisions of my Presidency!

My obvious choice was gone. Laurie had graduated the previous year. I had a number of options. There was Stephanie Erb, who was one-half Janis Joplin and one-half sophisticated debutante. Steph was a tough-talking broad. But she had her tender side. During my first year at the Academy, she and her sidekick, Bunny Eakins, would spend the night with Judy and me at the apartment when Mom needed to be in Steubenville. I had recently noticed that Steph had a "killer body." But I knew that Steph was too cynical to accept my invitation.

Another option was Carey Roberts, a sophomore. She was a lot like Steph, boyish in mannerisms, a "major partyer." Carey and I had already attended a formal dance held during Christmas vacation in Steubenville. We had a great time that night and she even kissed me goodnight on the lips, which instantly transformed her into another object of infatuation. But Carey and I weren't very close anyway and I thought that I had come on too strong ever since "the kiss." She had distanced herself from me. As part of my penance, I thought she would be happier going with someone else.

I chose Laura MacLeod. She had the sexiest nickname I had ever heard. People called her "Lolly." She caught my attention during 20th Century American History, taught by Richard Webster, the head lacrosse/basketball coach. He was famous for his Marine Corps demeanor as well as his "groupies," who were the most attractive and athletic girls in the school. "Lolly" had a dancer's lithe body with Suzanne Somers-like legs. Lolly wasn't shy about displaying them in her famous upper thigh-high mini-skirts. We traded barbs during Mr. Webster's lectures. She was witty and enjoyed my sarcasm. She was unattached and a person confident enough to not feel awkward about attending a dance with someone who couldn't.

She accepted my invitation. To be as independent as possible, I asked Jeff Childress to be my chauffeur for the evening. Although my parents needed to be there as guests of "El Presidente," I didn't want to drive to the Allegheny Country Club with them. I wanted everything to run smoothly.

Nothing did. From start to finish, the night was a disaster. When Jeff and I picked up Lolly, she said that she didn't want to go immediately to the Allegheny Country Club. She wanted to be fashionably late. For a half hour we drove around the hills above Sewickley to make our entrance a bit more special.

When we arrived at the portico of the Club, Mom was standing beside Dad with a crazed look on her face. She flung the back door open and yelled, "Where the hell have you been!"

I said, "We've just been driving around the hills."

She then slapped my face three times — once with her palm, then with her backhand and again with her open palm. She was furious.

Your father and I have been worried sick. We thought you were in a wreck or drove off a ravine. He's been driving around for the last half-hour looking for you. What were you thinking?"

"Mom, we're okay."

"But everyone has been waiting for you! The reception line can't begin without you and the band won't start playing until they're paid, and you have the check!"

Dad finally intervened. "Okay, let me get him out of the car, Mildred. We've got to get inside."

I felt awful and was terribly humiliated that Mom had reprimanded me in front of Laura. I tried to forget about it, but I didn't. I hated disappointing my parents and I knew I would hear about it when the dance was over. I was outraged that Mom was so out of control that she had "gangster slapped" me in front of my date.

When I got inside, everyone expressed their concern. I could tell that Mr. Cav was disappointed in me as well. That really hurt my feelings.

Adding to my grief, Laura was a less-than-attentive date. I could only "dance" to fast dances. Over the last three or four years, I had loved dancing in my wheelchair by moving my joy stick to the beat of the music. But when slow dances were played, I couldn't participate. Slow dances were what dances and proms were made for. Fast dances were relatively impersonal exercises in which each person expressed individuality. But "strutting my stufff" on the dance floor didn't come close to the romance, intimacy and physical contact of close dancing.

The Third Opinion

I tried to ignore it, but seeing my date with her arms wrapped someone else's neck was extremely painful. Dances were never easy. I felt my most disabled at them. I wished that I wasn't in a wheelchair during these intensely personal and physical interludes.

On Prom Night '74, Laura spent not only most of the slow dances with someone else, she spent most of the night away from me. I felt that I deserved more respect than that. She had agreed to be my date.

Ironically, to hold a prom had been my idea. It sounded so good. It turned out to be a major personal catastrophe. Everyone else had a great time. All I remember are the double slaps in the face that I received from Mom and my date, one literally and the other emotionally. Prom became a four-letter word and it still makes me feel like running away.

There was only one final act remaining for the Mikita administration. As Senior Class President, I was designated the only student speaker at graduation. Five minutes were all I had to convey the spirit and vision of our class. Not a lot of time. But I felt that I could pull it off if I made every word count.

I had learned the importance of word choice and the power of vocabulary from Mr. Webster. He was both scholar and coach. He was physically striking – short, cropped blonde hair, a ruddy complexion and muscular build. His intellect was just as impressive.

At least once a day I would see him at the library table preparing for his classes. Webster began each class by writing a thought question on the blackboard, which would be the writing assignment and discussion for the next class. The thought questions were no longer than fifteen to twenty words. Nevertheless, Webster was such a wordsmith that he would labor over every word while seated in the library. Words, he taught, should not be spoken or written lightly. Thus, one must painstakingly choose the proper word to accurately and precisely communicate his thoughts. Webster spent a lot of time teaching my friends the fundamentals and fine points about basketball and lacrosse. I have always been grateful that he taught me the power of words.

Naturally, he was one of my editors when it came time for me to draft my commencement remarks. Mr. Webster offered several suggestions on organization and word choice, but he left the theme and content to me. I began the speech by using a metaphor named Mr. Graduation, who had intruded upon our community and was forcing all of us to leave our protected, comfortable lives. I enumerated our individual talents and the qualities that could be found in "our world." I spoke of sincerity, honesty, love and concern — that would be "the luggage" for our journey into the new world.

I told the audience that our class harbored no prejudice towards minorities. I said, "I am such a minority. Stereotyped by your great new world, Mr. Graduation, as being unfit to be part of everyday life, this stereotyping was shunned by my classmates. Through their love and acceptance of me, a member of the minority has become part of the majority." I ended my remarks by saying, "When we look back at this little world of ours, we will agree with Kurt Vonnegut, when he states in one of his satires, 'it was all so sad, but it was so beautiful.'"

Everyone leapt to their feet and gave me a long ovation. Besides their applause and my diploma, I received the Social Studies Award for my academic excellence in matters of history and current events. What meant the most was knowing how profoundly proud Mom and Dad were. For a brief moment, I paused and reflected on everything that had preceded this occasion. When Mom said, "We're so proud of you, son," I immediately declared "But Mom, I haven't done anything yet." There was another mountain in the distance that I had already begun focusing upon. Its name was Duke.

Chapter 16

It was never a question whether I would go to college. The issue was where. During my adolescence, Dad talked about the University of Pittsburgh. Since most classes were held in a skyscraper known as the "Cathedral of Learning," Pitt did not pose the architectural barriers that the majority of college campuses did in relationship to my wheelchair. But Dad also added, "Mommy can go to school with you. I'll get you two an apartment in Pittsburgh and you both can go to Pitt together."

That statement stoked my biggest fear; having to depend on Mom to attend college. I dreaded the thought of rolling into each classroom escorted by my mother. I knew that her presence would have an alienating influence on my ability to make friends and integrate into the classroom. With Mom in-tow, I would be misperceived as a "Mama's boy" and as someone who was immature.

Throughout my education, I had proven that I could succeed and thrive without her beside me. If she hadn't attended grade school, junior high, and high school with me, what made her so indispensable to my college plans?

College was my first opportunity to show everyone, including Mom and Dad, that I could live independently from them. That wouldn't happen if I went to Pitt or, as an alternative, Ohio State. I wanted to be out on my own and I knew that what I needed to do was to go away to college. Ohio State and Pitt were in my own back yard and too convenient for Mom to be a co-ed again.

The whole notion of Mom helping me in college was in conflict with my parents' approach in raising me. They encouraged my independence from, not dependence on them. Dad always said, "We don't want you to live with us when you're older. You need to go to college and choose a profession where you can earn a good living. Mommy and Daddy aren't going to live forever; we're going to die one day. We won't be here to take care of you. You need to live your own life."

Dad wasn't being morose, just typically candid and realistic. Although I knew enough about my muscle disease to believe that they would both outlive me, I still dreamed about living away from home, going to college and graduate school, and pursuing my career plans with my parents' support. But, from a distance.

I reminded Dad of his advice when we began discussing college in the spring of 1973. I told him that I could have gotten into either Pitt or Ohio State if I had stayed in public high school at Wintersville. It only seemed logical that since I was in prep school that I try to get into the best school possible. My grades were competitive with the top students in the country, and I felt as though I had done the right things extracurricularly as well. I had never settled for second best in anything else. I had to at least try. Mom and Dad agreed. Dad told me, "If you try and fail, then at least you know that you gave it your best effort and you don't have to live with the regret that you didn't have the courage to try."

FDR had attended Harvard. That was before he had contracted polio, but that was of little consequence. I recognized the power and prestige that accompanied the name Ivy League. So I visited and was interviewed at Harvard and Columbia. I was hopeful and excited about the possibility of getting accepted at either school. Harvard was more of a long shot and I discerned that my Harvard interview was more obligatory than meaningful.

The interview at Columbia was more stimulating, but the campus was cold and inhospitable. It struck me as too urban and I knew that living off-campus and living in New York City would be disqualifiers, even if I were accepted. I had learned that lesson several days before when we were in Boston.

Besides being interviewed at Harvard, I was interested in Boston University. I thought that "B.U." was a safe fall-back in case I wasn't Harvard "material." The day following my interview at Harvard, we drove to B.U. I was prepared for a city campus, but it felt like more city than campus.

Not surprisingly, the Admissions Office had steps leading up to it. I was prepared to confront access barriers at every school that I

The Third Opinion

planned to visit. None of them was built with wheelchairs and persons with disabilities in mind. That was part of the allure of visiting the type of schools that interested me.

I liked being a pioneer. The fact that people hadn't thought of me or considered the need to include me in their plans, had never deterred me in the past or discouraged me from pursuing my goals. I would have missed a lot of life, not to mention America, had I waited for both to become barrier-free. My life was about confronting and overcoming barriers. Buildings don't discriminate; people do.

Boston University's Admissions Office was at the top of a winding staircase. I assumed that my interview would take place in another office on the first floor. I never got the chance.

An admissions staff person came down the stairs with a look of horror on her face. She said, "Mr. Mikita, I'm terribly sorry. I didn't know you were in a wheelchair. You should have told us. We have no place here for you at Boston University. I could interview you and you could apply, but even if you were accepted, we would have no way of taking care of you and no place to put you. I wish you had let us know that you were in a wheelchair. There's no point in interviewing you."

I could not believe that I was hearing these words. They stung me. I was demoralized and humiliated. I felt inferior to other prospective applicants. My interests were subordinate to others simply because of my wheelchair. It marked one of the first times in my life that I felt powerless in the face of discrimination. It was very hard to conceal my feelings from this individual who was denying me a full and equal opportunity to compete.

After I dried my tears sitting in the car, the rage and the anguish lingered. Sure, there were other schools that would be more accepting of me and more compatible for my wheelchair, but that was irrelevant to this experience. The fact was that I deserved a chance to be considered on my ability and intellect, not excluded because of my disability.

B.U. didn't care who I was as an individual. It feared what I was sitting in. I told Mom and Dad that universities and colleges should be the leaders toward equal access and opportunity for everyone regardless of their disability. Then Mom said, "Well, this is why it's important that we're doing this. By visiting these schools, we're raising their awareness about students like you who deserve to be educated.

Hopefully, Boston University learned something this morning."

Evidently it did. In less than ten years, Boston University became known as one of the most accommodating and accessible universities in the country for students with disabilities.

In addition to Harvard and Columbia, I was extremely interested in Georgetown University, particularly its School of Foreign Service. Again, I knew I might be the victim of the numbers game. I had a high Grade Point Average and was in the top ten of my class, but I did not score particularly high numbers on the SAT. Consequently, I looked elsewhere.

Mom and Dad suggested that I look at Southern schools, especially Duke University in Durham, North Carolina. Not only were they concerned about my health in relationship to the harsh winters that would confront me at Eastern schools, they were more familiar with Duke than the other schools on my list of prospects.

During the summers of '71 and '72, Billy had attended "Bucky" Waters Basketball Camp at Duke. Coach Waters, head coach at Duke, had long been a favorite in my household. Before coming to Duke, Waters coached the West Virginia University basketball team — my parents' alma mater.

Towards the end of every camp, my parents and I would fly to Durham to watch Billy play in the final game that was played in the hallowed, cramped confines of Cameron Indoor Stadium. However, Duke was fourth on my list behind Harvard, Columbia and Georgetown.

Dad disagreed. So did Mr. Cav. They both stated that Duke, being comparatively smaller than my other candidates — only 5,000 undergraduates — was intensely competitive and known as "the Harvard of the South." That got my attention, but I still reserved my best recommendations for my top choices.

I asked Mr. Hertrick, my favorite English teacher, to write my recommendation for Duke, realizing that I never got an "A" from him and thus his recommendation would not hurt, but would probably not help either.

I also applied to two other schools in the South — Emory University in Atlanta and Vanderbilt University in Nashville. As a shoo-in school, I applied to Hofstra University on Long Island because I liked the name and Hofstra had recruited me to apply.

My parents and Mr. Cav were concerned that I had not applied to the two "wheelchair" colleges — the University of Illinois in Champaign-Urbana and St. Andrews Presbyterian College in Laurinburg, North Carolina. Both schools reportedly featured "ideal" barrier-free environments for students with disabilities, especially those using wheelchairs. Not only were their campuses entirely accessible, but they also provided attendant care and modified dormitory rooms for the students requiring it. It sounded too good to be true.

I decided not to request an application from either school. I told my parents and Mr. Cav that if I did attend one of these wheelchair "utopias" for four years, that would only delay my inevitable transition into the real world, where neither the architecture nor the attitudes were so uniquely tailored to my needs.

Attending either Illinois or St. Andrews would further "handicap" me when it was time to live independently and without the help of such a sensitive and progressive environment. Eventually I would have to learn how to manage and structure my life in a society, which at that point had largely ignored those of us with physical disabilities. Since I wanted to leave home anyway, now was a good time for me to begin addressing issues of access and attendant care that would always be my responsibility and concern. My college experience, therefore, should prepare me to cope with all aspects of my life, including living in an inaccessible world. College needed to be just as tough as life. I didn't apply to either wheelchair school, much to my parents and Mr. Cav's chagrin.

As the rejections from Harvard, Columbia and Georgetown came rolling in, I began questioning my decision to not follow their counsel. But then one afternoon in March 1974, I came back to our apartment in Sewickley. Dad telephoned and said that I had received a letter from Duke University and I was accepted. It was a sunny, spring day, but after that news everything got brighter. Following my acceptance to Duke, I also received positive responses from Vanderbilt and Emory. Finally, Hofstra also accepted me a week after mailing my application

Duke was, from an academic standpoint, the best of the group. But the decision as to where I would ultimately go did not depend on academic criteria alone. I also needed to consider which of the schools would be most compatible with my wheelchair.

In May, 1973, Mom, Dad, and I traveled to all three southern schools to answer the question. I was so excited to know that I was visiting schools that had accepted me on my merits and the strengths of my high school performance. I felt like a basketball or football standout who was being heavily recruited from three schools. I felt sought after and needed. But that was all fantasy.

We first checked out Vanderbilt. The terrain was flat, but the person with whom we visited didn't appear at all enthusiastic about the prospects of my attending Vanderbilt. He did know of one particular dormitory that was off-campus and in a high-rise that might be suitable for my concerns. But, he pointed out, that was reserved for married students.

The thought of living amidst married students clashed with my idea of a college experience, but I had to keep an open mind in light of the fact that Vanderbilt had not had many students in wheelchairs. When we arrived at the high-rise, I immediately got discouraged. It looked so stark and desolate. I couldn't imagine living in such a place. The rooms were as antiseptic as a hospital. At that point I wasn't a big fan of country music so I wasn't upset leaving Nashville and heading for Atlanta.

I was greatly impressed with Emory. Located in a posh suburb of Atlanta, its campus featured sparkling white stucco buildings with red rococo roofs and beautifully landscaped quadrangles. However, I was surprised to find that the campus was on hills, and not as flat as I had expected.

I was even more surprised that the person with whom we visited was not very helpful in answering questions about where I would live and who could be enlisted to take care of my ADL's — activities of daily living. He did not know of any dormitories close to campus that would be accessible. But what I really felt was a sense of aloofness from him, an attitude of "this is your problem, not ours, so you and your parents deal with it." Emory, like Vanderbilt, was off my list.

When we got into our car, Dad immediately began reassessing where we were with the benefit of 20/20 hindsight. "Steve, you have to begin being practical. These schools aren't equipped to handle you and your wheelchair. You should have applied to Ohio State and Pittsburgh, like I suggested. Mommy can go to school with you and help take care of you. You just have to face the fact that they have never met anyone like you."

I didn't respond. I just couldn't accept that he might be right.

The Third Opinion

Maybe I had to resign myself to the reality that leaving my parents and going to a prestigious college was simply out of the question for someone like me.

Mom had a different response. "Well, let's not give up hope. All it takes is one, just one school that is willing to help us provide Stevie with a good education. Now is no time to panic. We have one more school tomorrow. Maybe Duke is that one school. Maybe it will be different. Let's not lose faith. We must remain prayerful and trust that God will lead us to the right place. He has never let us down yet. It only takes one."

When we arrived at Duke the next morning, I was dreading another rejection, just another administrator who would alienate us. Our first stop was the Admissions Office, where we visited with a woman who was very interested in me, and not dismissive about my needs. She couldn't answer with certainty many of our logistical concerns, but unlike those persons at the other schools that we previously visited, she believed there were answers at Duke. She said that she had taken the liberty to make an appointment with the Associate Dean of Student Affairs, James E. Douthat. His office was located on the West Campus in the Allen Building, Duke's main administration building.

When we got into his office, we all instantly liked Dean Douthat. He was extremely attentive. He wasn't intimidated by my wheelchair. He then amazingly said, "I have done some thinking and checking around campus, before ya'll got here. There is a dormitory here on West Campus that has an elevator. It's the only one on campus that does. We are willing to bevel any curbs that you need beveled in order to get to and from classes and to and from your dormitory. We will provide you with your own parking stall, just right outside your dormitory so you can park your van there."

"You're the first freshman in a wheelchair that this school has admitted in its fifty year history. We want you to come to Duke. As far as people taking care of you, I will talk to our work study program to find out if we can assign you a roommate that can help in meeting your daily needs. When its time to register for classes, we will have the Registrar hand-carry your class selections, rather than putting them through our computers. That way, when you have chosen a class that is scheduled in a building that is inaccessible, we will assign that class to an accessible one, so you can get into it without any problems. I'll stay in touch with you and your parents through the summer to work out the details. We're glad to have you here at Duke. You're going to love it."

We already did! I was going to Duke University. Mom was right. It only took one! Just one individual who looked at me as an exciting challenge, not an insurmountable obstacle. Just one person with the energy and courage to embrace me, all of me.

It would have been so easy for Dean Douthat to not take the time, not care, not to make the effort. But he didn't. Instead, he gave us his vision of what the Duke experience could be. His vision contained the details that mine had lacked concerning how we would tackle this next challenge from a practical standpoint. He was so confident and calm about matters that were so critical to my sense of independence and security.

Douthat was the epitome of the Southern gentleman — soft-spoken, charming and polite. But in his eyes and heart there was an intensity and clarity of purpose that Mom and I felt that very first day. With tears streaming down our faces, we said good-bye to Dean Douthat.

As we strolled out of the Allen Building, we saw the famed Duke Chapel at the center of the campus with its Gothic spires shimmering in the bright sunlight. Mom said, "Let's go to the Chapel and say a prayer of thanksgiving. We have so much to be thankful for."

I was thankful for my parents and for Jim Douthat. I was thankful for Duke University, for giving me a chance and providing me with the opportunity to start on this new adventure. It only takes one and we had found it.

It was another victory. I was going to college on my terms and in my way. I didn't need to compromise or be practical. This was a dream for which I had fought too long not to come true.

Chapter 17

In August 1974, Dean Douthat telephoned Mom and said that he had found a roommate who was willing to be my primary care giver. He, too, was an incoming freshman, named Philip Ayivor — a foreign student from Ghana.

It all sounded so exotic and collegiate. But I had plenty of worries — not about my performance in the classroom, but about my physical needs and living conditions. When freshman orientation week began, these concerns escalated.

First, Philip had an extremely small, unathletic build. He struggled to lift me. He had a lot of desire, but no skills or instincts to care for me. I could quickly see that it was going to take much patience and training for me to feel comfortable with him.

Second, I couldn't believe how loud the other freshman that lived around me were. Stereos were blazing at all hours and my room was located right off the elevator on the first floor. Since my hospitalizations, I had become extremely sensitive to noise. Mom purchased a sound machine that made a soothing ocean-like hum to block out external noises. She also bought earplugs to block out the noise further. But neither my sound machine nor my earplugs were any match for the heavy thumping of the bass sounds emanating from every other student's room.

Third, I was annoyed by the lack of privacy. Not only was I unable to nap in the afternoons due to the blare of stereos, but also I couldn't get used to the common bathroom. The fact that there was always someone else in the bathroom, when I showered or used the toilet, was quite traumatic.

Dad reassured me that this was just part of college. I would get used to all these things. But they were causing me fatigue and anxiety. Doubts began creeping into my mind that maybe I really wasn't cut out for college. One thing I felt good about was that Mom said that she couldn't leave Durham until I felt confident and secure. I could tell she was a little worried, too, but we had endured a lot together and college wasn't as hard as a hospital or oxygen tent.

What kept us both sane during those first few weeks was my sensitive and seasoned orientation group leader, Paul Stavros. Paul, a junior from Clearwater, Florida, was a real "Dookie." Paul was very accessible to both Mom and me. Nothing was a major problem. When I would take myself too seriously, he would say, "Get over yourself, Mikita!"

I envied how at home he was at Duke. I never thought I'd achieve that degree of stability about my living situation. Mom said just to be patient and persevere.

Her advice was echoed by the University's Minister, Reverend Robert Young, at the Duke Chapel in an extremely moving sermon given on the first Sunday of school. Young, known as one of the most dynamic and gifted preachers in the South, was an extraordinary orator, who understood inflection, pacing and thematic simplicity, like no other speaker I had heard.

On that particular Sunday, Young reassured the timid throng that we needed to recognize our feelings, and not suppress them. Over and over, he repeated the piercingly, poignant refrain, "Okay, I'm scared. I'm scared, but it's okay." Those words were what I was feeling. More importantly, I wasn't the only one feeling them.

I wasn't any different from my classmates. I wasn't alone. I stopped believing I was the only one who was frustrated and afraid. As Mom explained to me, right after the sermon, most college freshmen experience difficulty and challenge. "Just because you have different concerns than they do, does not mean that you should feel guilty about your fears and doubts." In other words, we may not be in the same boat, but we were all on the same stormy sea — being a freshman at Duke.

Besides training Philip, it was obvious that Mom and I would have to expand our helper network to a greater extent than we ever had before. I required help with showering and dressing in the mornings and assistance in getting in bed and turning me over during the night. But now I needed assistance in a host of new areas.

I needed help just walking to my first class every morning. This required finding someone who had the commitment to meet me at the same time on every assigned morning, gather my books in my book bag and escort me down the elevator. Then escort me to my class. Once I arrived in class, the person would place a notebook on a table, so that I could take notes.

When class ended, another person would need to walk with me either to my next class or to the Perkins Library, where I would study at one of the long tables in the Grand Reading Room or at an unassigned carrel in the stacks.

At the noon hour, another classmate would meet me in the library and accompany me to lunch in the Union Building. Then, following lunch, we would return to my dormitory room, so that I could use the bathroom and then, off again to the library, for more studying until I returned from the library to take my afternoon nap at 4:00 p.m.

Following my nap, I would need to be dressed again, lifted back into my wheelchair and taken to dinner at the Union. Then we would go to the library for an evening of studying.

Finally, at 9:00 p.m. or 10:00 p.m., I would be escorted back to my room at Buchanan and lifted in bed.

Because of the strained relationship that I had endured with Ronnie during my rehabilitation from the spinal fusion, I knew that relying on a single attendant or a couple of attendants would be much too confining. Plus, I feared that the more time I spent with someone, the more likely that I would be perceived as a burden to them. By involving thirty to forty people, i.e., fellow students, both males and females, I would benefit from the personal interaction with a variety of people. They were less likely to view me as someone who was demanding more of their time than they were willing to give.

In my first semester, my supply of helpers came from two main sources — Paul's friends at Buchanan and the Student Employment Office. Among the most helpful of Paul's contacts were Dick Calvert and Paul Juraschek. Besides taking me to dinner and studying, Dick and Paul, concerned about my sleepless naps and restless nights due to the commotion outside my first floor room, volunteered to trade their spacious, isolated third floor room for mine.

They had waited their turn on the seniority ladder to move into this exclusive third floor corridor that featured only three dorm rooms: two double occupancy rooms and one single occupancy room. This wing of rooms was separated from a stairwell and another corridor by two heavy fire doors that sealed off the corridor from traffic and sounds. An extra attraction was that, being on the top floor, I did not have to worry about footsteps and stereos above me as I had on the first floor.

Their act of charity was physically and emotionally liberating. Now I was able to sleep during my naps without dreading insomnia. My room became a sanctuary where I could retire each day to rest and reflect. I felt in control again.

When I wanted social interaction, it was only a couple of fire doors and an elevator away. Also, the bathroom was much smaller and more private. I didn't feel so vulnerable, and at the times in the morning and in the evening when I used it, rarely was anyone there. In fact, we placed my dressing table there as we had in our Sewickley apartment to facilitate my dressing.

Through student employment came students who either needed extra spending income or who were interested to aid someone with a disability for the practical, clinical experience. I would speak with the candidates by phone and conduct a preliminary interview to ascertain what their major was, their class schedule, any prior experience helping someone with a disability, their ability to lift me and their sincerity. Then I would schedule an in-person interview.

The personal interview was principally designed to see what their reaction was to me. I could determine by looking at their body language and their eyes whether they were comfortable and mature enough to help someone like me. One fatal flaw was if the interviewee spent an unusual amount of time looking at my wheelchair or my hands while I spoke, rather than looking at my face and eyes.

I would review with them the information that they had given me over the phone in order to give them a chance to elaborate. I emphasized that this was not a typical job. I told them I wasn't interested in someone who approached this as just another way to earn money. I explained that there were other more lucrative opportunities if that was their motivation for applying. True, they would be financially compensated for their duties, but the money was little more than spending money — $10 for a shower or $5 to put me in bed each night. I wasn't interested in mercenaries.

What I was offering was an experience to learn about me and an invitation to become involved in my life. In return, they would be getting a number of benefits. Aside from the money they would earn or the meal that I would pay for, I offered them a friendship. I told them that I was down-to-earth, well-rounded, witty and emotionally supportive. That is what this opportunity to help me was all about — having a relationship. Love and loyalty would drive it, not time clocks and money.

I knew this was a risky proposition. Most of the students I talked to came from extremely well-to-do families. They were relishing their freedom and independence. They had heavy class loads and crowded social calendars. Now I was asking them to include me in their lives, to think of my needs rather than theirs, to be responsible for someone else. I was out on a limb but I had to be. The alternative was to go back to Ohio, live with my parents and assume a sheltered, hermetic life.

I couldn't finesse the fact that I needed their help in order to stay at Duke. Yet I had enough faith in the human spirit to know that there would be individuals who would respond positively to my request. I also had confidence in my ability to attract helpers. I was courteous, polite, and sensitive to their time constraints, but the most critical consideration was that I knew I had a loveable and unique personality. I could laugh about myself and life. I was a good conversationalist. I knew they would like me.

People gravitated towards me. Once a student began helping me, one of his or her friends would express interest in being included in my life and schedule. Word-of-mouth became my greatest resource after my first semester.

Some days I would have my doubts. Thankfully, Mom hadn't left. "Don't lose faith, honey," she would admonish. "God has always blessed us with good people to help us take care of you. This is going to take time. But, don't worry, God will guide them to us."

She would say a prayer for both of us and I would remember those days as a thirteen year old struggling to breathe out of one lung in the lonely mist of the oxygen tent. Invariably, the telephone would ring and it would be another student who had read the advertisement that Mom placed on the bulletin board in the Student Employment Office, or a friend of a friend would express an interest in becoming involved. Mom would say, "See, I told you so, there are good people wherever we go. With God, nothing is impossible."

It took about a month, but then it was complete. Mom said it was like running a small business. Mom would graph my schedule on legal pads and compartmentalize every class, meal, nap, study time, morning wake-up and dressing and nighttime responsibilities. Thirty to forty names a semester would fill the time slots. It was staggering in its detail. But it worked successfully. It provided me with variety and flexibility and did not require too much responsibility from anyone. Still, there were anchors, a couple of people I could depend on, whenever someone forgot to show up or was ill.

For that first semester my "surrogate" Moms were Paul Stavros and Kevin McCafferty. Kevin, ironically, was from my hometown, Steubenville. He was the same age as Billy and had attended grade school with him. Kevin had a smaller frame than Paul, but as an ex-high school wrestler he had no trouble lifting me. Both Paul and Kevin were pre-med majors, and thus they were academically as well as emotionally inclined to help me.

With Kevin and Paul heading up my staff, it was time to allow this network of love to grow. That meant having to say good-bye to Mom to see if I could do what we had always dreamed and talked about me doing.

I never knew that it would be so painful. I was scared and Mom was distraught. During the other tough challenges and trying moments of my life, she had been there to comfort me or strengthen me or both. She seemed not only sad, but lost. Our lives and souls had been so inextricably linked that it seemed she had never planned for what came after this. What would be her role? How would she spend her time? What would be her focus?

It was hard on me, but so much harder for her. I could see it in her eyes, and feel it in her hug. We sobbed. She was afraid, not just for me but for her, too.

For the first time in my life, I felt sorry for her and felt the burden of her grief. She said, "We've raised you for this moment. You know I wouldn't be leaving you, if your father and I didn't think you could do it. You've always been our brave boy. There are so many people here already who love you and worry about you, especially Paul and Dean Douthat. If anything goes wrong or if you need me, I'm only a phone call or one hour plane ride away. I am so proud of you. You're at one of the finest schools in the country. Now, it's time for you to shine. You know how much I don't want to leave but I must, my love.

The Third Opinion

I love you and will miss you so much."

I said, "I love you, too, Mommy. I'm going to miss you."

I so much wanted her to know that, like never before. I was overcome with a feeling of humility and gratitude for all she had done, all she had said and all she had meant to me — always.

I felt that I had never adequately thanked her. I realized that she was not only my mom, but also an extraordinary woman of vision, tenacity and courage. She was not only worthy of my love, but the world's admiration. She truly was a remarkable woman. I realized that I could not have reached this stage in my life or attained anything else without her. She was my treasure, and not the other way around. I was proud to be her son.

For the last eighteen years I had been bathed, fed, held, turned over, dressed, taught, disciplined, spanked, consoled, exhorted, praised and adored by greatness. But I now knew it, and I wanted her to know that I knew it.

There were so few words and so much emotion. All I could muster was a whimpering, "I love you," as she blew kisses to me with her customary radiant smile, and then closed the door to my dormitory room.

Then I cried harder and longer than I ever had in my life for me, for her and for us.

Chapter 18

Once my helper schedule was set and my routine in place, I was free to devote more time to my studies. I knew that I could not take a heavy class load that first semester, since the physical aspect of my life would require a lot of my attention. I took English Composition, required of all freshman, as well as European History and Introduction to Philosophy.

All three classes offered their unique features. English Comp. was held in a cavernous lecture hall. There were at least 150 students in the class that was taught by an eccentric-looking and Oxfordian-sounding instructor named Williams. His lectures were as captivating as they were fun. The teaching assistants, who reviewed my assignments, were helpful and patient.

I was surprised that my papers contained a number of red marks, indicating that I was not the accomplished writer that I believed I was. I could tell that "A's" would not come easily at Duke.

European History, albeit a freshman course, was a seminar with only fourteen students. Initially, I was reticent to participate, since I was intimidated by the elderly professor, who seemed very rigid and humorless. I loved the subject matter of the course and enjoyed the viewpoints of my classmates.

Introduction to Philosophy was taught by another old professor. The upper classmen called him "Easy B" Negley. Negley never smiled and didn't refer to notes during his stream-of-consciousness lectures. His reading assignments were obtuse, but at least I knew that I would get no less than a "B" in the class, if I showed up.

The highlight of my first semester wasn't the classroom, but the choir loft. I had been accepted into the Duke Chapel Choir, after auditioning during orientation week. The Choir Director was Benjamin Smith who was demanding and zany.

Each Wednesday, following dinner, I would have to be lifted up several levels of stairs into the Duke Chapel for a 90-minute rehearsal. We would rehearse again for 30 minutes prior to the Sunday worship service. I was proud to be a member of such a glorious-sounding choir. Smith's anthem selections and interpretations were truly angelic.

The most thrilling event of my first semester was the privilege of singing Handel's "Messiah" in five standing-room-only performances during the first weekend of December. Each performance left me both physically exhausted and emotionally exhilarated. Even my worry about exams dissipated during these musical interludes.

I received all "B's" for that semester. I was disappointed that I did not attain an "A" in any course, but recognized that a 3.0 wasn't damaging in the long term, especially in light of my preoccupations with my daily needs.

As soon as I returned from my Christmas vacation, I caught the flu. Mom and Dad, who had accompanied me back to Duke to help me complete the helper schedule, took me to the Student Health Center. Following my examination, the female physician, out of my earshot, castigated my parents for subjecting someone with my disability to such a stressful environment as Duke University. She told them that they should rethink their decision to keep me at Duke. She advised them to take me home to Ohio, where I could stay home and be protected from the rigors of campus life.

Dad took her advice very seriously. My reaction was just as serious.

There was no way I was ready to scrub this mission. Of course, Duke was synonymous with pressure. But I could handle it. I was still adjusting to college life. All I needed was time. I promised that I would get to bed earlier and take longer naps in order to conserve my strength and not get run-down. I knew that Philip, my roommate, said that he was no longer interested in rooming with me, but there had to be an alternative to just throwing-in-the towel. I really hadn't begun to fight. I pleaded with Mom to intervene with Dad. He agreed to not give up on this experiment, for the moment.

My future at Duke hung in the balance. Mom understood how

desperately I wanted to stay. She said she was out of ideas, all but one — Dean Douthat. Mom told him that Dad and she were concerned about my health and my ability to maintain my stamina. She also said that she didn't know how to meet this latest crisis — who would stay with me at night.

Douthat, as always, had the solution. Crises were his job as Associate Dean of Students. He was constantly assisting students experiencing academic, financial and social difficulties. He never panicked. His approach to problems — all of them — was always the same: methodical. He told Mom that it was not uncommon for freshmen to come back from Christmas vacation with either a cold or flu. He said that I had performed ably in my first semester, in light of the other aspects of my life that required so much of my attention and energy. He didn't believe we had bitten off too much.

As far as the second problem, that, too, was not insurmountable. Douthat said he was planning on raising the issue with the Interfraternity Council that met weekly under his supervision. He also said that he had thought of another student on campus who raised funds for the last two years as Duke's Campus Muscular Dystrophy Association representative. His name was Jim Tompert. He lived in the dormitory next to mine. Mom said she would call Tompert and make an appointment. Douthat said that he would have news from the Interfraternity Council the following morning.

The next day, Douthat reported that the representative to the Council from Sigma Phi Epsilon, Chip Chamberlain, stepped forward following the meeting the night before and said that he and his roommate would be willing to help me at nights. Chip suggested if Douthat could identify two other guys willing to share nighttime responsibilities, then it would not be so overwhelming.

Each pair of helpers would be responsible for two weeks of nights per month. Douthat told Chamberlain that his idea was worth exploring and that my mother would be meeting with Jim Tompert the next afternoon.

Mom returned from her meeting with Tompert with the same commitment. She described him as serious and studious. He had asked a lot of questions about me, but there was definitely a tenderness about him. Tompert told her that he had lost his mother when he was a young boy, so he appreciated what we were struggling to achieve at Duke. He also said that his best friend, Rick Vilkin, would be willing

The Third Opinion

to help him in splitting the nighttime duties.

Douthat had worked his magic again. He wanted me to stay at Duke as much as I did. His *ad hoc* problem-solving approach was not only impressive, but worthy of study. As someone who had always been disabled, I had taken pride in my ability to improvise and to implement ways of accomplishing things that were individually tailored to my abilities. For example, I used a coat hanger to turn on or off light switches that were not otherwise reachable from my chair, or bit into the index finger of my right hand to keep my head from falling backwards whenever my manual wheelchair was tilted backwards to negotiate stairs or a curb, or had my morning helpers turn the hot water on at a very low intensity, so that the water temperature wouldn't fluctuate so dramatically, every time someone would flush a urinal or commode or use another shower or sink.

Before I met Dean Douthat, I thought that inventing new ways or different ways of doing things was a uniquely personal responsibility. Now, because of Douthat, there was another person in my life, besides my immediate family, whose input, advice and ideas were helpful. Douthat welcomed these challenges and looked forward to developing a strategy or plan to tackle the next problem on my horizon that I could not always predict or foresee. As a result, I felt less stress about making personal decisions, without Mom and Dad's help. I had access to someone who found the laboratory of my life intriguing and a valuable learning experience. Douthat bolted to the head-of-the-class in "Mikita 101."

With the two pairs of night helpers set, I fell in love with college. It was everything I had dreamed about: great classes; fabulous professors; intellectual discussions; late nights at the library; study breaks at the Union hang-out known as the Cambridge Inn; and shooting the bull in my room every night with one of my night helpers as I snacked on Pringles, peanut butter, green olives and Oreos.

My night helpers were better than any single roommate could have been. "Chip" Chamberlain looked like he had stepped out of a Land's End catalogue. He was dashingly handsome, articulate and compassionate. His father, Charles, had been a Republican Congressman from Lansing, Michigan, for twenty years.

Chip needed me as much as I needed him. He wasn't sure he wanted to follow in his father's footsteps and go to law school. He vacillated between being a gung-ho frat boy to questioning whether he really was deriving any benefit from the fraternity. He was afraid he was losing his long-time girlfriend. He valued my advice and counsel. I was flattered how much he sought me out. He quickly became my best friend.

Jeff Quaritius was Chip's sophomore roommate. "Q," as everyone called him, enjoyed everything about the Duke experience — except studying. The son of a Florida insurance executive, "Q" constantly talked about his lack of motivation, but never seemed to do much about it. Rarely was he moody.

Most of our discussions involved either the fraternity parties or Q's summers spent off the Florida coast on a fishing trawler. There was no doubt, however, regarding his commitment to me. On the second night that he ever stayed with me, Q demonstrated his vigilance.

In the middle of the night, one of my wall posters came crackling down. Startled, Q believed that I had fallen out of bed. I heard him yell my name and then I heard a loud thump and muffled moan. I asked him what happened. He said, "Steve, as soon as I heard that noise I started running towards your bed. I forgot that I was zipped into my sleeping bag. I tried to run, but obviously I didn't get far. The thump was me falling face down on the floor." Q and I could not stop laughing for the rest of the night.

My second pair of night helpers was an odd couple. Jim Tompert looked like a young Republican and had one of the deepest voices I have ever heard. I loved his analytical approach to everything. The only thing he felt passionately about was Duke basketball. He was extremely mature for his age. Every time I would complain about a class or become obsessed about some co-ed, Tompert would chide me to become more logical and less emotional.

Jim's best friend was Rick Vilkin. Hailing from Los Angeles, Vilkin, a senior, redefined California cool. With his unruly mop of hair and year-round tan, Vilkin looked like a surfer dude. He was laid-back and yet extremely sensitive to all my needs.

A notorious ladies' man, Rick was less impressed with a woman's appearance and much more interested in her mind. Vilkin was either too confident or cynical to be overly concerned about anything. He spoke in soothing tones and was always ready to discuss my recent predicaments. He, like Q, distinguished himself in the annals of my night helpers.

One night, Rick, who had a steady girlfriend, apparently did not want to leave her in his room. After I had fallen asleep, he invited her to join him in the helpers' bed, which was no more than six feet away from mine. Two or three times that night, Rick awoke to turn me over. I never suspected that Rick was also entertaining someone between turns. His secret would have gone undiscovered, if not for my morning helper's disclosure. I wasn't surprised or that angry because Rick was that cool. What chutzpah!

My night helper arrangement was like having four roommates. But it was also as if I lived alone. My room was my space. I didn't have to share a closet, wall, or refrigerator with anyone. When the telephone rang or there was a knock at the door, it was for me. If I needed privacy or desired company, it was my choice.

My second semester grades showed I was making the adjustment. Two courses in particular fascinated me: Introduction to Political Science, and The New Testament. Political Science was a likely major and the professor, Arturo Valenzuela, made that a greater likelihood. It didn't hurt that I received an "A."

The New Testament was more of a surprise. Duke had a Divinity School that not only trained future ministers and preachers, but also featured world-renowned theologians and professors who not only offered courses to the Divinity School graduate students but also taught undergraduate courses.

My New Testament professor, James Charlesworth, was enthralling. What intrigued me most, however, was the way that Charlesworth would dissect a single passage from the Bible and surmise why the writer chose to include it within the chronicle of Jesus. Charlesworth introduced the class to a new way of studying religious texts. After taking Charlesworth, I began seriously entertaining the thought of becoming either a minister or theologian.

Chapter 19

When school began in the fall of 1975, I was still struggling with the question: What will I major in? And just as importantly, what will I do with my major following graduation?

I had a third option: Majoring in Political Science, not as a primer for law school, but as a career itself. I was taking an introductory course in American Foreign Policy from Professor Albert Eldridge. I began calculating the pluses and minuses of getting a Ph.D. in Political Science and becoming a university professor. All of these options were intriguing. I consulted with Chip, Rick, Jim, and Dean Douthat. They all gave the same advice. Just enjoy all these possibilities for the time being; I was only a first semester sophomore. The choice would eventually become clear. Besides, we had more important things to talk about — women.

I loved telling my night helpers and Dean Douthat about my latest crush. Sometimes they knew something about "her." My informants would relay such data as year in school, major, boyfriend, sorority and whether "she" resided on West Campus or East Campus.

There was a co-ed who had fascinated me since my freshman year. She looked different from the other women on campus. I would usually see her walking between classes or through the dining hall. People knew of her, but very few knew her. That was frustrating.

I really wanted an introduction, but no one I knew was close enough to her that I felt comfortable asking to arrange a pre-meditated, but spontaneous-looking, meeting. I had gotten only as far as an occasional "hello" as we passed by one another. She was an enigma.

The Third Opinion

I couldn't get over the fact that an entire year had come and gone and still I had never met her or had the opportunity to speak to her. That was rare. I had been successful as a freshman in becoming friends with practically every other woman that had interested me. She eluded me and everyone else.

A year's research had revealed that her name was Susan Lundahl. She was a gymnast, which accounted for her chiseled figure and v-shaped back. She had a blonde, pixie haircut. She was a junior from St. Petersburg, Florida, and lived on East Campus. She was the Alpha Tau Omega fraternity's "little sister," which meant that she hung out with Duke's football player fraternity.

There was something about her that I just could not forget. She appeared independent and self-assured. I never saw her with anyone. She was always alone. That gave me hope that she wasn't dating anyone seriously.

However, I was definitely intimidated. She was a jock, and I assumed she spent a lot of time with jocks. I concluded we were not part of the same crowd. Still, I couldn't get her off my mind.

I had already spent an entire year trying to get to know her. I wasn't willing to wait any longer. I had to make my move. Now or never. Put up or shut up. I couldn't rely on anyone else to intercede on my behalf. I had exhausted every lead, with no success. I decided to take things in my own hands. I had no other choice. It was a bold but risky move.

If she weren't nice or if she had a boyfriend, that would end everything, including my fantasy that we would meet one day and go out on a date. That was a lot to lose.

But my curiosity was fueling my courage. Usually, I would enlist the help of a friend to approach a particular girl and express my interest in getting to know her. That way if she weren't interested, I would be spared the embarrassment and rejection.

Another equally effective strategy to meet women was simply seizing an opportunity to get to know a girl in class, in the library, or at the cafeteria. I would ask for assistance gathering my books, pushing an elevator button, or carrying my dinner tray. Then I would exploit that benign contact into a dialogue about a class or professor. That strategy worked flawlessly with everyone, except Susan Lundahl.

I couldn't depend on a friend or fate to bring us together. Sue wasn't subject to the rules of engagement that had produced other friendships. It was all up to me.

It was a Friday afternoon in October 1975, one of those Carolina days that tempted you to cut your afternoon classes and just sit out on the quadrangle and either people-watch or throw a frisbee. I nervously picked up the phone and asked the operator for Sue's number.

I didn't think she would be in her room. But I was ready, if she did miraculously answer. I had rehearsed my lines repeatedly over the last several days. A female voice picked up the phone on the second ring.

"Hello?"

"Hello, may I please speak to Sue Lundahl?"

"This is Sue."

"Sue, I don't know whether you know me; this is Steve Mikita — the guy in the wheelchair on campus."

"Oh, yes, I know who you are," she said matter-of-factly.

"Well, I hope this isn't presumptuous of me, but I was wondering whether I could take you to dinner one night next weekend."

"You're not being presumptuous at all, but I do have a boyfriend. So, I can't go to dinner. How about if we go to lunch, instead?" she suggested.

Disappointed that she was already committed to someone, I swallowed hard, and said, "That would be great! What would be a good day for you?"

Sue said, "Thursday?"

"Thursday is good for me. Would you mind stopping by Buchanan? I'm in Room 314."

"Not at all."

"I'll see you then."

"Okay, thanks for calling."

It hadn't turned out as I had dreamed, but she hadn't totally rejected me. Lunch wasn't romantic, but at least Sue had not said no entirely.

She sounded confident on the phone and had been honest. She was a person who didn't mince words. She was decisive, too. That intimidated me.

Our Thursday lunch was disappointing. Sue was abrasive, especially when she asked, "So how long have you used the wheels?" I was taken aback by her characterization, but I plowed ahead anyway and described my medical history from the time of my muscle disease's onset to my bout with pneumonia when I was thirteen years old.

She was interested but not mesmerized. We exchanged typical information. I learned that she was a psychology major. John, her boyfriend, was a lacrosse player. She wasn't going to compete in gymnastics any longer. She lived on West Campus now, in one of the new dormitories just down over the hill from my dorm. She was very smart and driven.

Regrettably, we didn't connect. There was no chemistry between us.

When Sue walked me to my dormitory, I was relieved lunch was over. She didn't say, "Let's do it again." She thanked me and said that we would see each other around. Then she was gone. My feelings had changed.

I definitely wasn't infatuated any more. I wasn't so sure I was interested any longer.

We exchanged a couple of "hellos" over the next month, when we bumped into each other. But Sue was still so aloof. I never thought we would ever be more than acquaintances.

Yet she was a challenge and her character and moxie were alluring. Those factors, plus, her palpable sexiness, were worth another lunch.

It was the Friday before Thanksgiving, 1975. It was rainy. I was going to leave for home that evening and cut my classes the following week in order to get a longer vacation. My friends said that's what everybody did. I was excelling in the classroom, so why not define my vacation on my terms?

I was in a good mood. But my motorized wheelchair was being repaired and I was in my push chair. I called Sue to see whether she could help me go to lunch. Surprisingly, she said she would be right over.

She showed up wearing a rainslicker and a smile. We connected the moment she walked through the door.

She was extremely helpful in wheeling me to the Union, dodging both the raindrops and the cracks and crevices of the sidewalk. We really enjoyed each other. She had a playful giggle and a caring heart. She wanted to know more details about my life. She asked about my childhood. She told me that she admired me and that it took "balls" for me to be doing what I was doing, i.e., going to Duke. She was sensitive and perceptive.

I never wanted lunch to end. It was one of the rare times in my life that I didn't care whether it was raining. My intuition about Sue was right. Sue Lundahl was as special as I dreamed she would be. We were becoming friends.

When we returned to the dormitory, she told me to call her after Thanksgiving, so we could go to lunch again. Then she grinned and her blue eyes disappeared. My interest in her was rekindled. I've never looked at those boxy, yellow rainslickers the same since.

Chapter 20

When January came, it was time for Mom and me to fill out my helper schedule. One slot was open and I thought it would be ideal for Sue. Every Thursday at 2:00 p.m. I needed to go to my private voice class at the new Music Building on East Campus. Marty Trover, a pre-med major, had been my Thursday afternoon helper the previous semester. But Marty could no longer help me because she had a conflicting class. I asked Sue if she'd be interested. She said that she was very interested, but she had to check her schedule to see whether she could commit. She telephoned the next day and said she would do it.

Thursdays became magical. Sue would meet me in my dorm, we would go to lunch at the Union, and then drive to voice class. Sue would either read in the van during the fifty minute class or drive to the nearby convenience market to get a drink.

What made our afternoons special, however, was what transpired after voice class. Most of the time, we would loiter in the back parking lot of the Music Building. Sometimes, we would return to West Campus and sit on the quadrangle. If the weather was bad, we would sit in my van. In other words, it didn't matter where we were because it seemed we were always alone. It was as if the rest of the world didn't exist. That's how intensely intimate our relationship was. I had never experienced this with anyone. Sue and I talked about everything — from the existence of God to fraternity keggers. She wanted to know everything about me. She invited me to share feelings and perspectives on things that no one had ever asked.

After awhile, I wanted every day to be Thursday. I couldn't believe that this relationship was so reciprocal. She gave as much as I did. That was a first. She cared as much as I did. That was a miracle. I was actually having a relationship with someone who loved spending time with me and who repeatedly verbalized it.

We devoted many Thursdays to talking exclusively about ourselves and our relationship. I never tired of it. I couldn't get enough of it. I had never felt so important and so fascinating to anyone, with the exception of my immediate family. If I were quiet for a moment, Sue would plumb the depths of my thoughts. I couldn't believe how much she wanted to know about me.

One afternoon I was feeling particularly frustrated because of the dull routine of my life. I told Sue that I wasn't happy on weekends. I felt I was the only person on campus not having fun on either Friday or Saturday nights. She had her boyfriend; I had no one. Everyone else seemed to either have a date or be involved in a relationship. Their weekends revolved around fraternity and sorority parties. Mine involved loneliness and isolation at my long table in the library.

Sometimes I was the only one in the Grand Reading Room for two or three hours. I was so lonely that I would pray for someone to come through those doors to let me know that I wasn't the only person at Duke that particular night that wasn't laughing, dating or kissing someone.

I told Sue that I resented the fact that girls were never physically attracted to me and that they never considered dating me. I was tired of friendships. I wanted to have a girlfriend. I yearned for the security and continuity of a romantic relationship.

It was hopeless. I was consigned to a life of studying and being alone. Sue listened to every word. She didn't interrupt. As always, she was totally focused on my feelings. It was the first time that I shared these thoughts with anyone.

She offered these thoughts, "Stevie, just because you're spending time in the library on Friday and Saturday nights doesn't mean that everyone on campus is happier and less lonely than you. People at fraternity parties may appear to be having fun, but a lot of them are more unhappy that you are. You know who your are, Stevie. You have direction in your life. You've always set goals and achieved them. Most of those frat boys and jocks don't know who they are, don't know where they're going, are involved in very superficial relationships and don't have the courage or honesty to admit that they're unhappy. They act like they're happy, when they really aren't, and then get drunk every weekend, so they don't have to deal with their feelings. You have misread them. You have to concentrate on you and all you have going for you. You don't need to compare yourself to anyone, especially jocks.

"I know a lot of football players. You're so much more interesting to talk to. Yeah, they might have better bodies than you, but you have things going for you that they don't have. You're very intelligent, you're sensitive, you're a good listener and you're fascinating. So don't be envious of them or feel as if you have to compete with them or anyone. Just know that you're not alone in feeling lonely and unhappy at times. Everybody does. I get lonely even though I'm dating someone. Some of us just pretend that everything is great so as not to deal with our true feelings. Our Thursdays together, Stevie, are a lot more beautiful than any party on a Friday or Saturday night. So don't think that you're missing out. You need to love yourself and recognize how wonderful you are."

Sue didn't have the 1960 copy of *Look* with her. But it was as if she had been there, when Dad delivered his soliloquy. Someone, other than Mom and Dad, had given me essentially the same advice. I couldn't change how I looked. I could control how I viewed myself in relationship to an able-bodied world.

Sue reminded me that I needed to value who I was. She defined my strengths, without minimizing my fears and frustrations.

I didn't have to party every weekend night, date someone or get laid to be happy. Sure, I was lonely, but not alone. That was an important distinction. I didn't suppress my loneliness nor did I pretend that I wasn't lonely. I admitted it.

At the same time, I had so many things to be grateful for. I had meaningful friendships and an ability to get in touch with my feelings and then articulate them. Most importantly, I had Thursdays with Sue. No one else on the Duke campus could say that.

Besides helping me understand who I was, Sue was also my mentor on love relationships. My initial infatuation with her had grown into a very deep love. I knew we would never be a romantic couple, however. Sue was in love with John. I longed for her feelings to change. I knew my dream would never come true.

Nevertheless, I could not suppress my possessiveness about her.

Sue encouraged me to share these feelings also. She said that she cared about me very much and that her feelings for John did not affect her feelings for me. She told me that just because her feelings were different for both of us, didn't mean I was less of a person or lower down her ladder of priorities.

She explained, "Love isn't finite. That means I can love everybody in my life as intensely as the other. Just because we don't have a physical relationship doesn't mean that you aren't unique to me. One of the greatest lessons you've taught me, Stevie, is that a person doesn't lose his dignity or their identity by asking another person for help.

"Before I met you, I was too proud to ask anyone to help me. Now, I know that depending on people doesn't weaken you but actually strengthens you and them."

Still, I would lose perspective and not be satisfied with simply being Sue's best friend. I wanted it all. I would try denying how much she meant to me by pursuing other women and fantasizing about these relationships. The fact was, however, that I had never felt as much passion for anyone as I did for Sue.

A couple of weeks before finals in the fall semester of my junior year, I experienced the simultaneous agony and ecstasy of being in love. Sue and I had spent the afternoon together but she was unusually quiet, practically noncommunicative. I repeatedly asked her what was wrong. She reassured me it had nothing to do with me or us. She said, "I know I'm being a bitch. I'm worried about finals and I'm concerned about my honors thesis in psychology. On top of that, I miss John. We haven't seen each other for awhile'

After voice class, it was obvious we weren't going to spend the remainder of the afternoon together. She just wanted to take me back to my room and be left alone. My questions were only exacerbating things. I really felt hurt and rejected. When we got back to my room it was as if we were complete strangers.

She said, "I'll see you later."

I desperately asked, "When will I see you again?"

Sue said bluntly, "I don't know". She then said, "Look, I really have to go."

I said, "Call me, if you need anything."

She only replied, "I have to go." Then, she slammed the door. I felt awful and so abandoned.

Ten seconds later, there was a knock at my door. Sue stepped in only halfway and declared, "I love you."

I replied, "I love you, too." My life changed. It was a defining moment. I was twenty years old and no woman outside of my family had ever spoken those words to me. I was in total shock. I felt alternative emotions of elation and despair. I couldn't believe it. I didn't know what to do with those words.

That's all she said and then she left. All I knew is that I loved Sue more than anyone, but I knew she wasn't in love with me. At that point, I didn't care. I loved her and she loved me. No words had ever affected me as much. I couldn't sleep and didn't feel like eating. That night, I vomited three times. I wanted to be with her, hold her, love her and marry her. I was embarrassed that I felt so wildly out of control. I tried to study or think about my ambitions or other relationships. That was futile. I could only think about her. I needed to talk to her.

The next morning, I called at about 11:00 a.m. and apologized. I knew how much work she needed to accomplish. She said she was heading to her office in the Social Sciences Building to input some research data on her professor's computer, but she had a few moments. I told her that I didn't want to annoy her, but that I was traumatized by the previous day's disclosure.

I told her I felt out of control since she had said those three powerful words. I told her how confused I was and that I had lost perspective. What terrified me was that I thought my obsession would drive her away.

Sue immediately allayed my fears. "Stevie, I will always be here. I'm not going to run away or end our relationship. You're too important to me and I need our friendship. I will do whatever you need me to do to help you regain perspective. If you don't want to see me for awhile or talk to me, I'll miss you but I'll be here waiting for you, when you want me to come back into your life. And don't feel badly about feeling the way you do."

Sue's reassurance taught me about trust and commitment in relationships. I didn't feel like I needed to walk on eggshells and that our future wasn't threatened every time I wasn't on the same emotional wavelength as she.

Two weeks later, on my twenty-first birthday, Sue and I went to dinner and then came back to my room. I had someone lift me into my rocking chair and Sue lay on my bed and read from the book that she had given me to celebrate and commemorate our relationship. The book was *The Prophet* by Kahlil Gibran and as Sue read her favorite passages about love and friendship, she placed our relationship on a spiritual plane.

I never read again *The Prophet* after that night. I didn't need to. Our bond could not be defined by even a poet like Gibran. It was that indescribability that made it so sacred.

Chapter 21

The following semester was the most frenzied of my college career. I was deluged with paper after paper. I could never choose Political Science over Religion, so I elected to double major.

My focus in Political Science was American Foreign Policy and in Religion, New Testament Theology. That semester was definitely my most rewarding and demanding.

I took the Reverend Barney Jones' course entitled "Christianity in America." "CA" was virtually a lock for an "A." No tests, no attendance requirements and no assignments. It wasn't for the faint of heart, however. There was only one formidable requirement — three thirty-page papers with a thousand pages of documented research for each paper.

There were two other courses that same semester that had equally grueling requirements. The first was the American Presidency taught by the legendary James David Barber, whose book *Presidential Character* used biography to predict and evaluate presidential performance in the White House from Taft to Nixon. It had catapulted him to national prominence and guest appearance on morning talk shows. Barber was no pushover. As he put it, in introducing his syllabus, "I don't give many A's. So, if you're not a serious student, this class could ruin your life."

Half of the students followed his advice and didn't attend the next class. I had been weaned on presidential character — FDR's. So it was going to take more than professorial bluster to discourage me. This was a chance to learn even more about FDR and be graded for it. Barber didn't ruin my life; he made my semester with an A.

The class that was truly a worry was my upper-level graduate seminar entitled American Foreign Policy: The Origins of the Cold War. It was taught by Ole Holsti, renowned for his prolific writings on the subject. Most of the students were master's degree candidates, but I held my own in our weekly discussions. That was confirmed by a special guest lecturer who came into class one day to share his experiences of the Yalta Conference that Roosevelt, Churchill and Stalin attended to map out Allied strategy. His name was Alger Hiss, then in his seventies but still the subject of national controversy.

In the late 1940's, Hiss was part of the Second "Red Scare" generated by the House un-American Activities Committee. A confirmed Communist spy, Whitaker Chambers, claimed that he had received correspondence from Hiss revealing State Department secrets. Before the Committee, which included Congressman Richard Nixon, Hiss testified that he did not know Chambers. The evidence proved otherwise. As a result, Hiss was tried, convicted and imprisoned for perjury. He always maintained his innocence, however, claiming that he was framed by Chambers and unjustly accused by the paranoid Nixon.

Of all the students around the table that afternoon, I had the most questions relating to Roosevelt's private agreements with Stalin, prior to Yalta. I also asked Hiss to describe the status of Roosevelt's health. Hiss told Professor Holsti after class that he was particularly impressed by my breadth of knowledge of this time period. What fascinated me most about Hiss was that he had actually seen the man whose life had inspired and helped define me.

In my seminar paper, I took a critical look at FDR the strategist. I analyzed both his public foreign policy, which the American people were given, and the private foreign policy that he had conducted with Stalin to secure the Soviet Union's commitment to assist the Allies against Japan.

The paper was only supposed to be forty pages. I telephoned Professor Holsti and told him that I had created a monster — 126 pages worth! He said he was excited to read it. Not as excited as I was, when Holsti called me to say that because of the paper, he was giving me an A+ for the class — a rarity at Duke. He also said he had nominated my "monster" for the Political Science Writing Award for Best Undergraduate Paper, which I subsequently won at graduation the following year.

The Third Opinion

Even before the class and award, Professor Holsti had a special place in my heart. Holsti's son, Eric, was the second freshman in a wheelchair that had come to Duke. Eric had Duchenne Muscular Dystrophy.

Tragically, Eric's health was deteriorating rapidly. He was extremely weak and emaciated. As a result, his mother had to attend class with him and escort him everywhere. Consequently, Eric, who lived with his parents in Chapel Hill, was precluded from integrating fully into campus life. He was shy and didn't make friends easily.

I talked to both Dean Douthat and Professor Holsti concerning my wish to provide Eric with a more complete Duke experience, that would increase his interaction with students. Eric's medical condition vetoed my suggestions. It also ended his life all too early. He died in his sleep one morning near the end of his sophomore year. Professor Holsti called me that same day to inform me of Eric's death and to thank me for my friendship.

I still think of Eric several times a year, whenever I am feeling pressured and overwrought. I say to myself: "Why are you feeling sorry for yourself? Eric wasn't given the opportunity and longevity to fulfill his dreams. He would have loved to be where you are. Stop pitying yourself, Steve. Go out and do it. Eric never had your chances."

One chance I was not going to miss, while at Duke, was the opportunity to leave the ivory tower and take part in the Washington, D.C. internship program. Washington had always energized me and now the internship gave me the chance to work on Capitol Hill.

Our Congressman, Wayne L. Hays, was extremely powerful. He was Chairman of the House Administration Committee and either punished or rewarded his colleagues by expanding or limiting their office space, supplies, mail privileges and travel vouchers. The day before I was to begin interning for Hays, *The Washington Post* broke a story that featured allegations from a Hays secretary, Elizabeth Ray, claiming that she was being paid primarily to have sex with Hays. Ray stated that she was unqualified to be anyone's secretary — she couldn't type and didn't know how to answer the phone.

With this chink in his armor, Hays was besieged by allegations of abuse of his power and privilege as a Congressman. Needless to say the first four weeks of my internship were spent reading *The Washington Post* and staying out of the way of investigators. Then, Hays had an aborted suicide attempt. One afternoon, he telephoned his Chief of Staff, Doug Frost, from an Eastern Ohio hospital where he was recovering. Frost assembled the staff around a speakerphone.

Frost said, "Hey Boss, how ya doing?"

Hays, in a raspy monotone, whimpered, "I just want you to know how sorry I am."

Frost replied, "Sorry for what? Don't you worry about a thing. Just get better and come back as soon as you can." Frost then had everyone in the room bellow a cheer of support for the fallen king of the House. Later disgraced, Hays was forced to resign his chairmanship.

The new chairman, Frank Thompson, a powerful, veteran Democrat from New Jersey, promised he would reform House Administration. I became friends with Thompson's office manager, Kathy O'Hara. Kathy gave me a plum assignment — to prepare a report for Chairman Thompson on the operation and responsibilities of the many subcommittees that Hays had created to provide added perks to his allies on the Committee.

My research and interviews of the subcommittees' staff revealed that nothing substantive was taking place. I shared my findings with Chairman Thompson. He, like Hays, was gruff, arrogant and ultimately, deposed. Several years later, Thompson was caught on camera, along with several other Congressmen, accepting bribes in exchange for favorable votes in the scandal known as ABSCAM. I suppose it goes without saying that my resume was subject to several revisions and deletions when it came to explaining that Washington summer!

Having my fill of corrupt politics for one summer, the next summer was spent in the lazy town of Laurinburg, North Carolina. I needed to fulfill a science or math requirement as part of the Duke curriculum, but knew that those courses at Duke were so heavily populated with pre-med students that to take such a course would threaten my grade point average.

I hadn't taken math since my junior year at Sewickley, so I began exploring science options that were designed for nonscience majors — courses known as "crips" that were embarrassingly easy and that virtually anyone could take without the fear of jeopardizing grades.

Most majors at Duke had one or two "crips." I found one in the Botany Department to fulfill one-half of the requirement. It was truly a "crip" that required only two hourlies and a final.

The Third Opinion

For my second science requirement, there were other "crips" that were available such as "Rocks for Jocks" (Geology) or "Physics for Poets" (History of Physics). However, these bastions of A's still intimidated me and the risk of getting a C in a "crip" motivated me to look at alternatives.

I learned that I could take a course at another college and transfer only the credits to fulfill my science requirement. My summer school options were narrowed to essentially one — St. Andrews Presbyterian College.

St. Andrews was one of the schools that my headmaster and father had wanted me to apply to for college. I balked because it was too ideally suited for my physical needs. It wasn't as appealing as a four-year institution, but St. Andrews was perfect for summer school. Not only did it feature a six-week intensive biology class for nonscience majors, but also the college, through the Federal SEATA program, provided personal attendant services to students with disabilities.

The dormitory at St. Andrews was antiseptic, and hospital-like. Each room had an electric hospital bed, nurse call light, and a huge walk-in shower. There were approximately fifteen of us in wheelchairs — the majority of whom were quadriplegics as a result of vehicular or diving accidents.

There were only two of us who had always been in chairs — "Bo" Alexander and me. Bo was witty, fun-loving and one of the jolliest souls I have ever met south of the Mason-Dixon line. Every time Bo would laugh his upper body would spasm, causing both arms to contract at the elbow. After a while no one noticed. That was simply, good ol' Bo. I loved him as much as his laughter.

Not since my grade school days had I been around so many students with disabilities. That took some getting used to. I feared that I would lose my identity.

I learned that simply because we were all sitting in wheelchairs didn't mean I needed to feel threatened. We were all individuals, no different from any other person. Just because we were in wheelchairs did not create some sort of bond among us. I liked some of the students and was not interested in getting to know others. The fact that we were in wheelchairs was no more significant than our eye color, hair color or shoe size.

The most intriguing aspect of St. Andrews, aside from the delightful ease of the class, was my attraction to two women in wheelchairs

— Sandy and Theresa. Both of them were positively gorgeous. Both were quadriplegics. They attended St. Andrews year-round.

Sandy was demure, a Southern belle. Theresa was a latter-day Daisy Mae.

My frustrations concerning dating didn't improve with either of them, however. They only wanted to be friends. I liked both of them so much that for the first time in my life, I seriously entertained the thought of marrying someone who was just as disabled as I. I considered the barriers such a relationship might create.

First, I would need to earn a healthy income to afford round-the-clock attendants. Second, privacy would be a problem; we would always need to have someone around. Third, sex would be another obstacle because of our relative immobility.

I was twenty-one and very inexperienced. I had only kissed a handful of women. Needless to say, alternatives to regular sexual intimacy were beyond me.

I knew all of these considerations were much too premature. Neither Sandy nor Theresa were interested in me as their boyfriend. That realization hurt as much as it ever had. I wasn't good looking enough for them. They weren't any different from anyone else. I was never seen as a romantic threat until Martha Mueller changed that.

I met Martha during my junior year at Duke, through a friend, Geno Scioscia. I knew Geno at Sewickley Academy. Geno was ruggedly handsome and popular with girls. I called him an Italian Clint Eastwood. As a member of the Pi Kappa Alpha fraternity, Geno was in a good position to meet some women that eluded me. One was named Andrea Griffis.

Duke didn't have many beautiful women. Andrea was definitely one of the few. Everything about her was alluring. She was blonde, tan and extremely sophisticated. She was unabashedly cosmopolitan. She was from New York City, vacationed in Switzerland and had done some schooling in Paris. She even walked like a New Yorker, swiftly and never focusing on anyone or anything. She was that protective and that beautiful.

"Andy" told Geno that she was interested in getting to know me. We began having Thursday night dinners together and then studying in the library. She was fiercely independent, but very sensitive.

Andy's father had been incapacitated and inconvenienced for decades with a debilitating kidney disease. She was quite comfortable, therefore, with someone with a disability who enjoyed cerebral conversation and a sedentary lifestyle. Andy and I spent many evenings sharing our writing assignments and discussing style and word choice. She was my first friend that taught me the gift of letter writing. Consequently, Andy, like words, has always been very important.

Andy's best friend, Martha Mueller, told Geno she wanted to get to know me. I didn't know who Martha was. Geno's endorsement was all I needed. She was even more than he had described. Her father was an independent oil man from Texas and her mother descended from Mexican royalty. If anyone had ever come from wealth and prominence it was Martha or "Martita," her Spanish name. Tall, curvaceous and a face that very seldom had any make-up on it, "Tita," as I called her, was a Duke dream girl. Everyone wanted to date her. But Tita was shy and oblivious to the stir she was causing in the fraternity houses, those citadels of the oversexed. She could not have cared less.

Tita did not acclimate to the superficiality of campus society. She desperately wanted to be taken seriously for her intellect, not her physical beauty. Few men ever did that. We talked about our parallel desires to be respected and accepted. Martha's beauty was as challenging to her as my muscle disease was to me.

Just as many in society stereotype persons with disabilities, so too do they stereotype physically beautiful people like Tita. She was always treated as an object of desire and not as someone with feelings and opinions.

We were two people who were getting to know each other. We were battling the myths and stigmas that accompany disability and beauty. Unfortunately, too many people never got beyond Tita's breasts or my wheelchair.

Andy told me one night that Tita thought I was handsome. I rushed into a classroom in the library, closed the door and wept. It was one of the most thrilling moments of my life. No one had ever told me I was good looking, besides Mom. More importantly, I believed it, because of Tita's sincerity.

Chapter 22

Besides the wonderful education and remarkable people, there was another aspect of Duke just as integral to my life and every bit as unforgettable — Duke basketball. There is nothing like it anywhere in the country.

First, the games are played in Cameron Indoor Stadium, which has a seating capacity of only 6,000 people. Second, the students have the prime seats that are usually reserved for wealthy alums at other schools. Third, the students that do attend never sit. I was the only one that did.

Students are constantly in a frenzy — mocking opposing coaches, vilifying the opposing teams' players and ridiculing the academic credentials of the rival college. It was so intoxicating that we hardly noticed that the team had suffered so many losing seasons.

In my junior year our fortunes changed. The new head coach, Bill Foster, began landing some top high school prospects. Duke started winning. That intensified everyone and everything.

I was one of the first "Cameron Crazies" long before Dick Vitale, the colorful commentator of ESPN, labeled the raucous crowd by that name. Whenever we would play the North Carolina State Wolfpack, we would heartily chant: "If you can't go to college, go to State," knowing that the Wolfpack usually had better athletes. Then, when the Maryland Terrapins and coach Lefty Driesell visited, three rows of students behind the Maryland bench would attire themselves in three-piece suits and skull caps and imitate the flamboyant Driesell's every rant and rave.

But absolutely nothing compared to the hostility we held for our arch rival, the University of North Carolina at Chapel Hill. One hour before every game with the Tar Heels, we would scream: "Go to Hell Carolina, Go to Hell." It got so venomous one Saturday night that the student body decided to point out a particular player's distinguishing characteristic. Whenever he was fouled and shot a free throw, 3,000 crazed Dookies would shout, "Look at Buckley's nose! Look at Buckley's nose!" We would do anything and everything to gain a psychological advantage. This was no ordinary rivalry; it was tantamount to *jihad*.

During my senior year, the Duke basketball team regained the national prominence that it had enjoyed in the 1960's. The long drought was over. Duke was back on top. With such stars as Jim Spanarkel, Mike Gminski, and Gene Banks, Duke advanced to the National Championship against Kentucky.

It was a magical season and each student, particularly, we seniors, felt as if we had invested so much into that team, that the loss to Kentucky didn't taint the priceless memories of that season.

I felt especially close to the team because I had taken the class, "Coaching Basketball," with all of them. Coach Foster taught us every aspect of the game — from marketing to setting a screen. I was proud that on the mid-term there were two highest grades in the class — Jim Spanarkel, Duke's All-America point guard, and mine. But my fanaticism for Duke basketball had its price.

One afternoon, towards the end of May 1978, a friend from the Registrar's Office telephoned and said, "Was that you they were talking about in the article in the Alumni magazine?"

I had no idea what she meant. She was laughing but it didn't sound funny. I asked her if she would locate a copy of the magazine and I would come over to her office. When I got there, she showed me an article entitled: "Duke Fans: Is it worth it?"

The tenor of the article was a discussion of the passion and venom that characterized the Duke student body's support of our team. The article began with this narrative "The young man sits poised in his motorized wheelchair, waiting for his chance. As North Carolina State's 7'2" center, Chuck Nevitt approaches the free throw line, the young man propels his chair forward and screams, "You're ugly, Nevitt. You're really ugly!" And then it ended with: "It was a bizarre vignette."

The writer was talking about me. Of course, it was me. I was the only student in a wheelchair. I had been slightly more creative in my criticism of Nevitt. I had actually said, "Hey, Nevitt, Barnum & Bailey are coming to town. They're looking for a guy like you."

After reading the article, I was mortified. I was even more humiliated, when I realized that my commencement speech was now on President Terry Sanford's desk with two other candidate's drafts for his selection of the student speaker at graduation. I wasn't selected. My speech was better than the one Sanford chose.

I'm not sure that anyone else made the connection from the article, but I knew I lived in a fish bowl, and because of my disability, I could not vanish into a crowd. Mom said I needed to live the life of a public figure. Not even Duke basketball excused poor taste.

When it was time to graduate, I didn't want to leave. I grieved my loss for weeks before we marched onto the field at Wallace Wade Stadium to receive our diplomas. I left one goodbye until the end. It was one of the hardest of my life — Dean Douthat.

As soon as I got into his office, I began sobbing. Controlled, as ever, he said, "We've had quite a ride. It doesn't seem like four years, does it? Seems like yesterday that you came in a scared freshman."

I said what I had felt since May 1974 when he opened the door to his office and in so doing opened Duke's door to me. "I love you, Dean Douthat. I'm going to miss you. I could not have done this without you."

"Oh, I have a feeling you would have without me," he said, humbly. We both knew that wasn't true. He sounded like he always did. Calm, comforting. But there was something in his eyes that I had never seen, but always knew were there — the teardrops of my champion.

As we flew out of Raleigh/Durham Airport that evening, Mom said, "Don't worry. You will find another great place like this. But let's reflect where we have come. The Admissions Office told your father and me when they accepted you that you would probably graduate in the middle of your class with a 2.75 grade point average. Four years later, you're one of the most popular students on campus. You graduated *magna cum laude* with a 3.5 average in a double major, no less. Then, you won the Political Science Writing Award on top of that."

I said, "We did it, Mom," and then I held that familiar hand that I had squeezed for strength for twenty-two years, as we soared into a higher altitude — law school.

Chapter 23

My decision to pursue a legal career was both a spiritual and practical one. It was spiritual because FDR was a lawyer. He had parlayed his legal career into a political career. He ran for public office in his wheelchair. I wanted to do the same thing: establish a name and reputation as an attorney, and then seek public office.

By contrast, Political Science professors, I believed, lived too cloistered an existence for me to envision becoming a politician from a college campus.

Also, my paternal grandmother, Susan Mikita or "Baba" (Slovak for grandmother) always said: "Stevie, gonna be judge." It had been such a part of my life for so long it felt like I was predestined to be an attorney.

From a practical standpoint, law school emerged as the only real choice. I had always had strong writing and rhetorical skills. I recall Mom telling me when I was ten, during a discussion of possible career opportunities, "You should think about becoming an attorney. You're constantly arguing with me. Lawyers get paid to argue."

Dad concurred wholeheartedly. He said it was a versatile degree. Once obtaining a law degree, he explained, I would acquire a host of skills that would equip me for a variety of jobs in business or politics as well as the law. Plus, attorneys, generally, had greater earning power than college professors and ministers.

Dad encouraged me to prepare for the future. After all, I had been disabled since birth; thus insurance would not pay for my costly living expenses and specialized equipment such as motorized wheelchairs and customized vans. I needed to make money. Lawyers made money. Being a professor or minister just wasn't practical. Being a lawyer was.

There was another reason that being a minister was no longer possible. In 1976 my summer in Washington, D.C., I converted from being an Episcopalian to being a Mormon. Mom had joined the Church of Jesus Christ of Latter-day Saints in 1960 when I was five. It took me fifteen years and a research paper on Mormonism while I was at Duke to discover that many of my beliefs were rooted in Mormon doctrine.

I knew my decision to convert would not be received favorably by my friends at Duke, but I could not deny the powerful feelings that I had about this set of beliefs in comparison to other religious institutions and philosophies I had considered.

I was not looking to religion as a "crutch" to help me accept my disability. I was much too skeptical and cynical to believe that my decision was a matter of blind faith or wistful musings. Quite to the contrary, this was a decision that was as much intellectual as it was spiritual. It was not something that was a passing fad or born from a single momentary need for a rational explanation of a chaotic existence.

My research paper of Mormonism simply confirmed beliefs that I felt I always had. I wasn't required to change my way of thinking or forsake an old belief system. My conversion was more of a natural evolution than an internal revolution.

No one coerced me or influenced my decision. I didn't care whether anyone scoffed at my decision; I was at peace with it. I always believed strongly in God and Jesus. I knew there were others who believed in these same things and there was a church that I could go to each week to worship, to meditate and to sing. My beliefs found a name and a home.

Finding a law school to accept me wasn't as easy. Once again, I aimed high. I applied to over twenty schools, including Harvard, Yale, Columbia, Georgetown, Stanford, Vanderbilt, Emory, Ohio State, UCLA and the University of California at Berkeley.

My grades and recommendations made me competitive. My LSAT scores, however, were fatally low. I had never performed well on standardized tests, but my two LSATs were embarrassing. In fact, the second time that I took the LSAT, my score was eleven points lower than the previous one. The chorus of rejections couldn't be far behind.

The Third Opinion

Mom reminded me of her "it only takes one" axiom. That was of little consolation when the one I really wanted was the first to say "no!" It was Duke. I was dumbfounded. If any school had reason to look behind my dismal LSAT's, I thought it would be Duke. Evidently, I was just another number and an expendable one at that. Not surprisingly, the other schools followed suit.

By late April 1978, I had been wait-listed at Emory and Vanderbilt and had yet to hear from Brigham Young University and Ohio State. I started thinking that I might have to take a couple years off and either work in Washington or pursue a master's degree in Political Science.

Before graduation from Duke, I decided to make an appointment with Duke's Chancellor, Kenneth Pye. Former dean of the Duke Law School, Pye was known throughout the country as a tough and talented administrator. He had appointed me to serve on Duke's Section 504 Task Force to monitor Duke's compliance with the newly-enacted Federal Rehabilitation Act of 1973.

Chancellor Pye asked what was the purpose of the meeting. I said, "Chancellor Pye. I haven't been accepted by any law school yet. I'm worried that I may be rejected by every one of them because of my mediocre LSAT scores."

Pye inquired, "How many are left on your list?"

I said, "Ohio State, BYU, Emory and Vanderbilt."

Pye asserted, "Where do you want to go?"

His candor surprised me; so did the implications of what he was saying. I answered, "Well, if I had to choose, I would say Ohio State or BYU."

Pye said, "Well, let's see who I know at those schools." He flipped through his American Law School Directory and came to BYU first. His finger stopped. "Gordon Gee, Associate Dean. Gordon and I went to Columbia together. I'll give Gordon a call and let you know what he says." That ended the meeting.

The next day I was heading to the library when I heard my name being called. It was Chancellor Pye. He waved me over to him. He said, 'Steve. I talked to my friend, Gordon Gee, yesterday afternoon at BYU. He said they would make a space for you at BYU. How's that sound? Is that okay?"

I was speechless. I thanked him profusely, and cried all the way back to my dorm to telephone Mom and tell her that she was right again. It only took one call from one law school buddy to the other. I was going to law school in a place that I had previously associated with a large lake and Donny and Marie Osmond.

As it turned out, I was more prepared for living in Provo, Utah, than I was for being a law student. I had seen the famous portrayal of the pressures of a first year law student in the movie "The Paper Chase." I thought that only happened at Harvard or Yale, not BYU.

I was wrong. I really felt like a stranger in an alien culture. The professors were anything but friendly. They were as inaccessible as they were intimidating. The subject matter — Contracts, Real Property and Civil Procedure — was worse. Positively boring and deliberately obtuse, completing reading assignments was sheer drudgery. Class time further confused, not clarified, questions raised by the cases.

The volume of information that one was asked to digest for each day was staggering. I couldn't keep up. I was spending so many hours in class that I didn't have enough time or energy remaining to read sixty to eighty pages per subject each night. I fell behind. That increased my stress that I would be called on to recite a case without adequate preparation. I was afraid that I would be humiliated, as several of my classmates had already been. Adding to my frustrations was the fact that I wasn't understanding the issues under consideration at the depth that my classmates were grasping them. I felt dumber than I ever had in my life. Law school was tailored to exploiting my strengths — writing and speaking. I thought I was logical. As a 1-L at BYU, I wasn't sure of anything, except that I was tired and suffering from low self-esteem.

I couldn't believe how competitive the students were. Duke was a top-rated school. Still, I felt as though I always had an edge as an undergraduate because I outworked and out-studied many of them. At Duke, I paced myself and chose classes which I not only liked, but also didn't require daily attendance or unreasonably lengthy assignments.

Law school was dramatically different. Everyone was motivated and brilliant. My entering class was the twelfth highest qualified in the country on the basis of LSAT's and GPA's. Not only were they as smart or smarter than I was, they required less sleep. They didn't take afternoon naps and most of them didn't leave the law school for meals. They brought their lunches or their spouses brought them. That was another difference. Most of my classmates were married and many already had children. They were older than I was by at

The Third Opinion

least two years, since the vast majority consisted of Mormon males who had interrupted their college careers to serve two-year proselyting missions.

I was the youngest male in a class of 155 students. Many of them were absorbing the material at such an impressive rate, I really began questioning my decision to pursue a legal career. I knew that law school would be tough, but not so physically draining and psychologically damaging. Many of the students were enjoying the experience. I hated it.

Much of legal education's rites of passage are so unnecessary and harmful to one's esteem and ability to learn. It is deliberately abstract, having little, if any, relevance to the real legal disputes that occur in the courtrooms of this country.

Surely the Socratic method, i.e., spinning out a factual scenario and asking a series of question to test a legal principle, has its place, but equally important are clarity and respect. By placing a human face on the law, students would understand the combination of reason and passion that define great advocates for justice.

Law schools in America are still out-of-touch — long on *logos* and short on *pathos*. They are educating technicians that can elucidate texts, but who do not touch the lives of those whom they represent. Being a good lawyer is as much about feeling as it is thinking. Good law students are just good thinkers who understand the rules of this game called law school.

No matter how much I disliked the game, I had to play it better than I was. That required swallowing more humble pie. I could not improve my performance in the classroom without being honest about my limitations and expectations. The class load was just too heavy. I had to cut back and carry a reduced load. Rather than take five courses like my peers, I could only take three.

The implications of that choice were discouraging, even depressing. With a lighter class load I would not be able to finish my degree in the usual three-year time frame. It would take four years and thus I would forfeit my chance to graduate on time with my class. Everyone said that didn't matter. I was comparatively young and what was another year, anyway? They didn't understand that my record would be broken.

Ever since kindergarten, I had completed every grade with my classmates. I had never lost ground to them, in spite of hospitalization, convalescence and illness. I was always able to catch up and still excel. But I had to be realistic. Law school was so much more physically rigorous than I ever expected. My health came first, as Mom always said. So I followed her advice; I opted for an abbreviated schedule.

The best thing about my first year in law school was that it ended and I had survived — barely. Making law review was now a laughable, not laudable, goal. What helped is that I saw a lot of others who were equally deflated and demoralized.

The only axiom that I had remembered was from Stephen Fuller, my Civil Procedure professor. Fuller, famous for his acerbic wit, said, "Law school is to be endured, not enjoyed. Those of you who enjoy it, should make appointments with a psychologist or psychiatrist because you are truly in need of help." That single statement placed my first year into proper perspective.

Another source of joy following my first year was that my older sister, Carole, relocated to Salt Lake City, which is only forty miles north of Provo. I took most of the credit for her decision to leave Pittsburgh where she was anchoring the news for an independent station, WPGH, Channel 53.

To add a couple more credits, I decided to remain in Provo for a session of summer school. Carole needed a vacation and a break from her boyfriend, who was a hybrid between being a '50's beatnik and '70's hippie. I invited her to Utah to see the majestic mountains and experience the summers the high desert climate offers. I suggested that she bring her video tape out and interview with the three network affiliates in Salt Lake City. The stations liked her as much as she liked Utah. She received offers from all three and chose the CBS affiliate, KSL, Channel 5, where she began as the arts reporter.

As soon as Carole got settled, I left for Pittsburgh. Because of my low grades, I couldn't get a coveted first-year clerkship, but I wanted some type of practical experience to counter the negative feeling I had about my first year.

I offered a federal district judge in Pittsburgh my services as a volunteer legal intern for six weeks. Judge Maurice Cohill, known as "Pinky" in Sewickley circles, was the father of one of my sister Judy's closest high school friends.

Judge Cohill reaffirmed why I went to law school. He gave me meaningful research assignments, allowed me to draft several opinions and sought my input. There was a wide chasm between the study of the law and the actual administration of justice that I witnessed that summer.

Judge Cohill inspired me to recommit myself to studying diligently, without taking law school so seriously. I could make a difference in the legal profession, even though I would not finish in the top ten of my class.

I returned the next fall knowing that I had not made a mistake — the law was the place for me even though law school wasn't. The reality of the courtroom more than made up for the artificiality of the classroom.

With a year under my belt and my sanity restored, my grades improved. Cynicism was another factor. I refused to be intimidated or to become obsessed about my studies, as so many were doing. I would do my best, but not lose confidence in myself or my goal — practicing law. What also helped was that I was taking a subject I liked, Constitutional Law. The professor represented the best of both worlds — scholar and lawyer. Rex Lee, the Dean of the Law School since its inception in 1973, was a gifted appeals lawyer. His insights into the Supreme Court fascinated me and my grade reflected it. I finally received my first "A" in law school.

Academically, my overall performance improved and I was demonstrating my practical skills as well. I received high marks in my moot court assignments and arguments before a panel of mock judges. I regained my confidence in knowing I had the right stuff to become a good lawyer.

In addition to the obsession of "making-the-grade," law students place a premium on obtaining summer clerkships. Law firms from throughout the country recruited at BYU with as much enthusiasm and interest as any top school.

Much to my surprise, I got as many interviews as the law review students. That meant that, at least on paper, I was an attractive candidate to law firm clerk hiring committees that sifted through the mountain of resumes. Each firm sent two or three lawyers on campus to conduct the interviews. My first-year grades were not a disqualifier. I was buoyed that those who had reviewed my credentials had considered more than grades and class rank — the primary factors that dominate recruiting decisions. I was excited with the prospect of clerking in New York, Houston, Phoenix, or Los Angeles.

Besides researching and drafting memos on important legal issues,

I looked forward to the courtship and schmoozing that would occur if a firm liked me enough to extend me an offer to join it following law school. Grades had not slammed the door. At least, I was inside and ready for what came next — the interview.

Each candidate was given only twenty minutes to make enough of an impression on the interviewers that they would justify a second look from the firm known as a "fly-back." These follow-up visits included an all-expense trip to the firm's headquarters — airfare, hotel room and meals. After meeting other members of the firm, the candidate would receive an offer.

I couldn't wait. Interviews were definitely something I looked forward to. I had distinguished myself on paper. I knew I could leave a positive impression on the interviewers.

I prepared for interviews just like an exam. Nothing was left to chance. I brainstormed questions that they would certainly be asking such as, "Why are you interested in our firm?" "What strengths do you bring to the firm?" "What area do you plan on pursuing in your practice?" "What distinguishes you from other clerk candidates that we will be considering?" "Do you know anything about our city and, if given the opportunity, are you sincerely interested in relocating?" "What are your hobbies?"

Besides formulating answers to these questions, I also prepared ones to interview them, such as, "What is the focus of your practice?" "What attracted you to the firm?" "Where did you do your undergraduate work?"

I also confronted another subject that my classmates didn't need to address — my disability. I knew that seeing me and my wheelchair would spawn many questions and concerns, not to mention fears, about my ability or inability to clerk at one of these major law firms.

I told them the nature of the disease. I reassured them that they were not interviewing someone who was a medical risk. I had outlasted many doctors' predictions of my demise and I had demonstrated my stamina and ability throughout my undergraduate and law school years.

I admitted that I could not work a sixty to eighty hour week, not unusual or unreasonable for law clerks and young associates. I could guarantee them only an eight-hour day. I would need to go home for a couple hours for physical therapy and a rest period. I was willing to work at home in the evenings and on weekends. I was a dedicated worker, I reassured them. The quality of my work would more than compensate for the quantity of time that I would spend on the job.

My candor was a two—edged sword. Addressing all of the questions that no one would actually ask me I believed would demonstrate my honesty and openness. I was not ashamed about who I was. I didn't want to pretend that the wheelchair wasn't there. Nor did I want them to leave Provo with an incomplete portrait of me.

Of course, such honesty carried the risk of scaring them off altogether. That's exactly what happened. As the interviews progressed, I sensed that none of the interviewers was willing to set aside their fears and prejudices about the disabled. They were outwardly friendly, but emotionally much farther away than the sofa where they sat.

My honesty got me nowhere. I didn't get close to an airport for those next two years. I only received icily polite rejection letters from every law firm that interviewed me. I didn't receive a single call-back or fly-back. They weren't interested in me. I really never was a serious candidate.

Large law firms are not like universities and law schools — they are businesses, first and foremost. They're not interested in making exceptions, understanding individual needs and accommodating disabilities. Their only purpose is to make money. That's why they are labeled "sweatshops." They seek strong minds and bodies to meet exorbitantly high "billable hour" requirements.

I thought I could break through this mind set. After two years of courtesy interviews and chilly smiles, I wasn't so sure that such a job was even worth fighting for. I didn't want to work with people who were so inflexible and shallow. I believed that Mom's "it only takes one" philosophy had met its match.

I could not scale the treacherous walls of this fortress known as the law firm. I was very distraught and felt trapped. How could I find a job if I couldn't find a clerkship?

My choices were dwindling. If I created problems for larger firms, there were even fewer chances that a smaller firm would consider me an asset. I was disillusioned with the legal profession. I no longer believed that law firms were places of tolerance and inclusion. Rather, they were stratified guilds with no commitment to diversity. I was determined to find a clerkship. I wasn't sure that there was another attorney anywhere that agreed.

I did find an attorney who was willing to give me a chance. He didn't work in a law firm, however. I met him in the Tabernacle on Temple Square in Salt Lake City.

I came to Utah in search of a wife. Instead, I found Orrin Hatch! It was the quickest job interview I ever had. It took no more than a minute.

At the conclusion of the weekly radio broadcast entitled, "Music and the Spoken Word," featuring the Mormon Tabernacle Choir, I asked Dad to push my wheelchair over to where Senator Hatch was greeting wellwishers. I said, "Senator, my name is Steve Mikita. I'm originally from Steubenville, Ohio, but now I'm a law student at B.Y.U."

Hatch responded with delight. "I think that's great. I'm proud of you. Why don't you come back to Washington, next summer, and clerk for me, be my law clerk. Just write a letter and remind me where we met. It's great meeting you."

"Thank you," I said. I believed him. Most politicians make promises that never materialize. I felt Hatch was being sincere.

He kept his promise. For the next two summers, I was his law clerk. When school ended in April, I would fly to Washington with one of my main helpers who would help Mom in setting up a temporary home in an Alexandria, Virginia apartment.

I couldn't believe that I was clerking for one of the most conservative senators in the country. Hatch, only four years into his first term, had already established himself as a powerful and sometimes angry voice for less federal government and more military build-up. I thought he was less likely to offer me a clerkship than any law firm. Thankfully, Orrin was a moderate on many social issues, including those affecting Americans with disabilities. I didn't want to be misperceived as betraying the disability constituency and its agenda by working for such an arch-conservative.

In my first summer clerkship, I was assigned to the Senate Judiciary Committee. Orrin had been a trial lawyer in Salt Lake City before running for office in 1976. The skills that he had honed in the courtroom were readily apparent whenever the Judiciary Committee held hearings and debated issues. Of all the senators I observed, Orrin was clearly the most dominant and well-briefed member of the Committee.

The Chairman of the Committee was Edward Kennedy, the legendary Senator from Massachusetts. I didn't see very much of him, however. He was immersed in his bid for the Democratic nomination. Kennedy was challenging the incumbent, Jimmy Carter who was losing ground in the polls to the Republican front-runner Ronald Reagan, Hatch's political hero. When Kennedy did make a rare appearance, he was ill prepared and obviously preoccupied.

One afternoon in June I was outside the minority offices in the Dirksen Building when I heard a rumbling sound that steadily got louder. I thought it can't be an earthquake; this is Washington, D.C. As the sound became deafening, I saw a phalanx of men marching in unison down the corridor. As they passed, I saw Senator Kennedy in the midst of them. With him nearly hidden, by the Secret Service agents, I thought that all of this protection was not only for him, but also because of who he was — the last, surviving brother of an American dynasty.

As his law clerk, I did not frequently interact with Senator Hatch, unless I had prepared a briefing packet on a judicial nominee that he was opposing or on a subject that interested him, such as the growing cancer insurance industry. I had more contacts and conversations with another senator that summer who went out of his way to speak to me at every Committee hearing or each time we saw one another in the elevator. His name was Bob Dole. I had always admired him and found his sarcasm refreshing. I felt comfortable around him because he was an American with a disability. Dole was wounded in World War II and, as a result, his right arm was paralyzed to his side. Dole was constantly needling me about Orrin's reelection chances in Utah and whether he really had any competition in such a Republican safe harbor. I reassured him that Hatch's seat was his for as long as he wanted it. Sure enough, Senator Hatch is in his fourth term.

Without a doubt the biggest thrill that summer was sitting next to Orrin at hearings on cancer insurance. The subject of the hearings was anything but exciting, but it was where the Committee met that took my breath away — the Senate Caucus Room in the Russell Senate Office Building. This was the historic room where the Senate Watergate Committee had met. I was sitting at the same table as the famous Chairman of the Committee, Sam Ervin, who characterized himself as just a "country lawyer." I wasn't intimidated sitting next to a Senator. I was humbled by that memorable marble room with its kelly green tablecloths.

The next summer I returned to "the Hill" and was assigned to the

Labor and Human Resources Committee, which had a new chairman, Senator Hatch. In the previous year's election, not only did Ronald Reagan evict Jimmy Carter from the White House, but the Republicans gained control of the Senate. Thus, rather than be in the minority, as the "loyal opposition," Republicans like Hatch would set the legislative agenda. Consequently, in 1981, everyone wanted to know what priorities Chairman Hatch would focus upon and bring to the attention of his colleagues. Orrin was asked by the Federal Labor Law Journal to outline his plans for the upcoming session. He asked me to ghost write an article that I entitled "The Senate's Repertoire of Reform."

At the end of this summer-long project, I asked that I be allowed to include a footnote in the article that would acknowledge my contribution. Hatch's Chief of Staff, Frank Madsen, said, "Orrin's never done that and he's not going to start with this article." That's when I decided I would not return following graduation to be one of Orrin's staff attorneys. U.S. Senators don't share the stage with anyone. I had not gone to law school to be content with sitting in the audience. I wanted to step into the limelight.

When I got back to Utah in late August, I was basking in the glory of a new role — matchmaker. For the last two and one-half years, it seemed that I was approached weekly by a classmate, who was interested in my sister Carole's dating status. Depending on who was making the inquiry, I would either say, "Well, she's dating, but isn't serious about anyone at the moment. Are you interested?"

Most of the time, I would paint a more discouraging portrait to protect Carole from having to go out with another underwhelming candidate. "No, sorry, she's very serious and contemplating engagement. Try someone else." But, one day, a second-year student, Paul Harmon, said that he had a promising prospect. He said, "I know this really cool professor that I would like to fix up with your sister." Staying true to my screening strategy, I asked, "Well, that depends on your responses to the following list of questions. Is he good looking? Down-to-earth? Good sense of humor, yet sensitive? Is he bright, but not arrogant?" Paul answered, "yes" to every question. I rewarded him with Carole's telephone number.

Nine months after that deal that was struck, I was attending Carole's wedding to Neil York who was not only the man of her dreams, but had become one of my best friends over the last summer in Washington.

The Third Opinion

Neil taught a summer session class at Georgetown, and we met most afternoons for lunch at the Madison Annex of the Library of Congress. He was researching an article on parallels between the Revolutionary War and the Vietnam War. I was delighted that Paul and I had brought two wonderful people together.

There was another romance, however, consuming my time and thoughts — my own. Before leaving for Washington, the previous semester, I met a beautiful and passionate undergraduate, Kim Summers. For me it was lust at first sight.

Our relationship began as most of my friendships usually did. I invited Kim to cook me lunch. The first thing I learned about Kim was that she was no cook.

But everything else about her was extraordinary. We talked, laughed, held hands and made-out. I was 24 years old and this was the first relationship that I could actually characterize as normal and romantic. It was incredible. I was dating someone for the first time in my life.

She was physically attracted to me. I had always dreamed and longed for such a relationship. Now, I was experiencing it, real intimacy.

We resided in the same apartment complex and so Kim practically lived at my place. We ate most dinners together. I either ordered-out or Kim had progressed to the point of warming up a can of split pea soup and mixing tuna fish with Miracle Whip. When she stayed overnight, she would either sleep on the floor beside my bed or in the other bedroom.

Some days she would shower at my apartment and we would talk as she dried her hair, put on make-up and dressed. We were a couple and I didn't think it could last. It felt too good and too normal.

After one of our passionate interludes, I looked into her eyes and told her how much I loved her for loving me and allowing me to love her. I said, "Kimmie, I can't believe that you find me attractive. I'm not nearly as handsome as you are beautiful. I feel inadequate. I really want you to be happy."

Kim said, "Don't worry. I'm very happy with our relationship. I am very satisfied. Shut up and kiss me." To be hugged and kissed by a woman produced a new feeling of acceptance that had eluded me.

I felt that I was fairly good-looking, but my body was not strong, nor athletic. I didn't look like those "jocks" in wheelchairs, whose upper bodies are as impressive as any other athletically inclined male.

There was no hiding the fact that I had never walked. I had spent my life in a wheelchair and my body looked like it. But that didn't matter to Kim. She loved both my mind and my body. It completed me.

All my life, until that point, people recognized my mind and praised my intellect. They rejected my body and ignored my sexuality or marginalized it.

Tita at Duke said I was good-looking, but now I was "sexy." That was altogether different. I wasn't being compartmentalized as so many women had done since I was sixteen. I wasn't just funny or a great friend. I was in love and being loved. I didn't need to suppress it or feel guilty about it. I just needed to express it and enjoy it.

Before Thanksgiving 1981, I looked at Kim on the couch. I drove my chair towards her, and reached for her hand. She asked, "What?" I dropped my head. She said, "What's the matter?"

With tears in my eyes and a tremor in my voice, I said, "I love you and want to spend the rest of my life making you happy. Will you marry me?" Kim smiled, and withdrew her hand.

"Steve, I don't know. I can't say yes right now. I feel like there's more for me to do and experience before I settle down and commit to someone. I'm not saying that I could never marry you. It's just not the right time."

She was right. It wasn't time and I was forcing something that cannot or, at least, should not, be forced. I knew she would say "no." But my insecurity and physical addiction to her had triggered my question. We were physically compatible and the best of friends. But that wasn't enough to form a permanent bond. We had differences, incompatibilities and disagreements on just about everything else, from raising children to Shakespeare.

When we returned from Christmas vacation, it was over. Kim said we needed to talk. She sounded more than serious. She began by saying the deadly, "I've been doing a lot of thinking lately about us." Then she dropped her verbal bomb. "I spent a lot of time doing things in California, you know, physical things, like riding bikes and going on hikes with my family. Those things are important to me. I want to continue doing them with my husband and my children. I have tried to act that those things aren't important, but they are and always will be. They are too much a part of who I am."

"Well," I said, "there's not a lot I can say, Kimmie. I'm never going to be able to ride bikes with you, go skiing or climb a mountain. If we were to get married, I would want you to continue doing those things and would support you doing them with our children. I can watch you do those things, but I can't do them."

"I don't miss not being able to do those things. That's because I've never been able to do them. I don't know what I'm missing, literally."

"Remember that night that you told me you dreamed about me walking? Remember what I told you? So many of my friends have had that same dream, but I never have. Not once. Walking is not part of my life, either consciously, or subconsciously. I have no idea what it feels like to walk. It's alien to me."

"I asked you to describe what it's like to get up out of a chair or how much energy you exert to get off the floor. You couldn't define it. There is really nothing in my life that I can compare it to. That's why I can't understand why physical activities, such as bike riding, running or skiing are so important to so many people."

"I can't comprehend how it is that people feel better and invigorated after they work out or the exhilaration they feel every time they race down a ski slope. When I exercise it's painful, frustrating and exhausting. I don't feel better. I feel disabled and weaker.

"I guess, what I am saying, is that if you are waiting for me to truly share in these physical activities with you, it's not going to happen. I can't, Kim. If you need someone like that, I am not that someone. I guess it's best that we both know that now.

"I think we could be extremely happy without me having to do all those things with you. My family's proven that. We spent vacations in big cities, going sightseeing, shopping and out to eat. What's important is not what you're doing, but the people who you're doing it with. I don't know of a closer family than mine and we never went on a hike.

"We come from two different worlds. I'm not saying that mine is better than yours. They're just different and neither one of us is going to change. I think it's time to say good-bye. This is not going to work out."

I was sorry that Kim and I weren't going to get married, but I didn't feel guilty that I wasn't the type of husband that she had envisioned. She needed to pursue her priorities and I didn't need to apologize for never having learned how to ski. I've always known a lot more about going up hills than down them.

Chapter 25

The same week that I proposed to Kim, I made another, more successful pitch for a job in the Utah Attorney General's Office. Carole went to the same church, in Salt Lake City, as the Deputy Attorney General, Paul Tinker. One Sunday Tinker invited Carole and me to speak during the worship service.

Tinker was impressed to the degree that he asked Carole what my plans were following graduation. Carole told him I would be very interested in working for the State. In addition to Tinker, Carole's best friend, Sharon Peacock, was an Assistant Attorney General.

On the Friday after Thanksgiving, I went to the Utah State Capitol Building which is a smaller version of the U.S. Capitol and located at the top of a very steep hill in Salt Lake City. Tinker said that, given my writing and advocacy abilities, I would be well suited for a new position he was creating in the Criminal Appeals Division. He explained that rather than prosecute or defend lawsuits in trial court, the focus of my practice would be the Utah Supreme Court, which was directly above Tinker's office on the third floor. He said that following their conviction, sentencing and imprisonment, increasing numbers of criminals were filing appeals. Their arguments ranged from insufficient evidence to illegal searches and seizures to ineffective assistance of counsel. Tinker said there was nothing more exciting than criminal law. Moreover, appellate practice was not as physically draining as trial practice. He recommended that we stay in touch over the next months until I graduated. He made no guarantees, but I knew that Paul Tinker was powerful enough to make my only job prospect a reality.

The Third Opinion

Following graduation I moved to a Salt Lake City condominium that overlooks the Forest Dale Golf Course in the Sugar House area, once known for its sugar refineries. I was so relieved to be out of a college dormitory and apartment complex. Finally, I did not have to worry about anyone's stereo or raucous parties.

However, one aspect of my life has remained the same. I depend upon a group of university students as I did at Duke and BYU to help me as personal attendants. It seems as though I am always training new helpers to learn my morning and nighttime routines. But the benefits of having young, energetic students around outweighs the frustration of constantly recruiting new ones to assist me.

As soon as I got settled in my condominium in May 1982, I had to devote the rest of the summer to preparing for the Utah Bar Examination. After enduring four years of law school, my future hinged on a three-day test. The first day was a national standardized test, known as "the Multi-State," and the next two days, consisted of essay questions emphasizing Utah law.

Every day, beginning in early May, I studied one of the twelve subjects covered on the Bar. In the evenings, I attended a live or video lecture at the University of Utah Law School. The entire process was an ordeal.

I was most worried about the Multi-state, in light of my history of disappointing performances on the SAT and LSAT. Standardized tests were not my forte.

The only accommodations that I requested of the Bar, prior to the test, were extra time for both the Multi-state and essay portions, as well as a separate testing room. These were the arrangements that BYU Law School provided me for exams.

I had never taken an exam of this magnitude and length, however. The Bar was helpful and sensitive to my concerns, but relied on me for suggestions since such accommodations had never been requested.

We agreed that I would be allowed an additional two hours for the Multi-state exam. For the essay portion, I was given one hour to complete each question rather than the standard forty minutes. That accommodation meant that my essays would spill over an additional day into Saturday.

Four days, twenty-four hours of testing and four sleepless nights later, I completed this grueling marathon. All that remained was waiting and worrying for the test results, which were announced two months later in September.

On the last Friday in September, I telephoned the Bar at the appointed time. I told the receptionist my name and she asked me to hold for Sherry Leeper who was in charge of Bar Admissions.

Sherry said, "Steve, I'm sorry, you didn't pass."

I immediately asked, "Did I fail the Multi-state?"

Sherry said, "No, your Multi-state score was fine. You failed the essay portion."

I was incredulous. "Sherry, that can't be true. I've never failed an essay exam in my life."

She responded, "Well, Steve, you needed to pass twelve and you only received passing grades for nine."

"Well, what do I do now?" I asked.

"Give me a call, Monday, and we'll discuss your options."

I was so embarrassed and humiliated. I was the only new hire in the Attorney General's Office who failed the Bar. It was an absolute nightmare. I had been through plenty of physical trials in my life, but now I was experiencing excruciating mental and emotional anguish. I felt the utter despair of being a total failure.

Nothing in my life had prepared me to confront the painful truth that I failed something I thought I was good at — taking essay exams. My self-confidence waned.

Paul Tinker was as dumbfounded as I. He suspected that something had gone awry and it wasn't because I didn't understand the material. My failure became a legal question. Tinker suggested that we approach this case like any other by conducting "discovery," i.e., gathering as much information and evidence as possible surrounding my performance on the Bar.

The first step was obtaining copies of the questions, my answers, and the model answers that the graders used in reviewing my responses. Secondly, Paul said that I needed an attorney to represent me, if we chose to appeal my results to a Bar committee. He said I would need to retain a private attorney to handle my case. Third, Tinker and the Attorney General, David Wilkinson, reaffirmed their confidence in me.

Sharon Peacock, Carole's friend, said she knew the perfect attorney to represent me. His name was John Meyers, Director of the Legal Center for People with Disabilities in Salt Lake City. Meyers was enthusiastic about my case and said that he would volunteer his services since it was publicly significant.

John gave me my first assignment to dictate the answers that I had given on the nine subjects that I had allegedly failed. He wanted to compare my answers to the graders' model answers to determine whether I had demonstrated my knowledge of the law. Next, John said he needed a medical opinion of my muscle disease, and what effects the stress and pressure of studying and taking the Bar had on my overall condition.

As I dictated my answers, I made a startling discovery. I couldn't read my own handwriting. Many words were illegible and the meaning of sentences was indecipherable. Coupled with this revelation, was a comment made to my brother-in-law, Neil, by a mutual friend, Ken Cannon, who had taken the test and had learned of my failure. Ken told Neil that one of his friends who was a grader had asked him whether there was someone who took the test who had a muscle disease. Ken said, "Yes. Steve Mikita." The grader said, "I couldn't read his answer, so I failed him." This was a major breakthrough.

A neurologist at the University of Utah, further bolstered our theory of the case — that my failure stemmed from my physical disability, not an inability to practice law. Dr. Fred Ziter came out of his office, shook hands with me and said, "You have Werdnig-Hoffman disease."

I said, "No, I don't. That's what the physicians told my parents when I was eighteen months old. They said I would be dead at the age of two. I'm nearly twenty-seven. How could I still be alive, if I had Werdnig-Hoffman?"

Ziter said, "I can tell that you have Werdnig-Hoffman because of the tremor in your hands. I have a lot of experience in diagnosing these diseases. You have the intermediate stage of Werdnig-Hoffman, which does not kill you as an infant, but puts you in a wheelchair. Given your age, you are in amazingly good shape for someone with this disease."

I told Ziter that the purpose of my visit was to ascertain what impact the Bar exam had on my writing ability. Ziter gave me a battery of muscle tests, particularly on my right shoulder, arm, hand, and fingers. He said, "It is scientifically impossible for me to explain how it is that you are able to write at all, let alone write for eighteen hours over three days for something so critical to your future as the Bar exam. Most people with your disease lose their ability to write when they're teenagers. It's a miracle that you can even hold a pen in your hand, due to its atrophied state. Why don't you dictate your work?"

I responded, Doctor, if I did that, then I would never be able to write again. Writing is what I do and what I love."

Ziter concluded, "The only thing that explains your ability to write is your sheer desire to do it. It's not only amazing that you're still writing, but also that you are alive."

Ziter offered his opinion about the detrimental effects that the months of study and worry leading up to the Bar had on my general health. "Steve, when able-bodied people are placed in a stressful situation, they have reserve energy to draw upon to help them meet the increased physical demands of the situation. They are not required to operate at 100 per cent of their muscle capacity on a daily basis.

"By contrast, you're always required to operate at 100 per cent muscle capacity, no matter what. When you're placed in a stressful situation, you have nothing in reserve. I can't imagine, after months of studying for the Bar, how your body wouldn't have been exhausted before you took the exam.

"If the Appeals Committee requires you to retake the exam in February, I will strongly recommend that you not take it because it would jeopardize your health. It would be foolish to subject you to this ordeal again. If you would like me to testify at your hearing, just give me a call."

After I shared Dr. Ziter's observations with my attorney, he had another thought. He believed that if my fatigue and stress levels were as bad as Ziter had indicated, then there must be some evidence proving that was the case. John said he wanted to determine when I was failing the majority of my essays, during the morning or afternoon sessions.

John also wanted to know whether my handwriting deteriorated as a result of the stress that made it impossible for the graders to read my answers. That question would require technical expertise that neither one of us had. John knew a handwriting expert, George Throckmorton, a highly respected investigator with the Salt Lake County Attorney's Office. John dashed off my essays to Throckmorton.

Throckmorton's findings were astonishing. He said in all of his years of doing handwriting analysis of extortion notes, suicide notes and other documentary evidence, he had never seen handwriting

The Third Opinion

that had deteriorated so dramatically over a short time span.

Throckmorton said that most individuals, when writing under stressful conditions, place a small percentage of their letters either above or below the base line. With the aid of magnified photographs of my essays, he explained that only a small percentage of my letters were above or below the base line at the beginning of the essay exam on Thursday morning. However, as the exam progressed, my stress and fatigue increased and my handwriting reflected it. A vast majority of letters fell either below or above the baseline and my writing became increasingly illegible, especially during the Friday and Saturday afternoon sessions. He said he had never seen such trauma in anyone's handwriting. John compared my answers with the model answers. He detailed how I had, in fact, identified the majority of issues on six of the nine failed essays.

With this evidence, John recommended that we make two alternative arguments to the Appeals Committee in mid-November. The first argument was that I had actually passed the essay portion of the exam. The graders could not read or did not read my answers. My dictated responses demonstrated that I had passed six out of nine essays.

John knew that the Bar, historically, was extremely reluctant to re-read essay exams. In fact, there were only two previous occasions in the 1970's involving class actions that resulted in reversals of failing grades. No individual had ever been granted such a reversal.

Accordingly, we needed another argument if the committee refused to re-read my essays. John found an exception in the rules governing such appeals. It allowed the committee to grant an appeal, if it would be a "manifest injustice" not to allow the individual to practice law.

On the night of my hearing, John and the rest of my supporters carried me up several levels of stairs at the Utah Bar Association. The fact that the office was inaccessible was discouraging.

Fortunately, the hearing was encouraging. My attorney methodically presented the evidence. Dr. Ziter described my disease and the debilitating effects that studying and taking the Bar had on my condition.

George Throckmorton illustrated how my handwriting had steadily worsened during the exam and that there was a correlation between the essays I failed and the time of day I wrote them.

Robert Parrish, who officed next to me, testified of my ability to practice law. Parrish said that I would be a gifted appellate advocate, if given the chance.

I was the last witness. It was the most important legal argument I ever made.

I said, "I'm thankful to tell you of my great desire to practice law in this State. But desire is only part of it. I also have the ability to practice law and to do it well. I have never failed an exam in my life, and I didn't fail this exam. Your reviews of my answers will substantiate that."

"I simply want the chance to serve others and better their lives. You will not regret your decision, if you allow me that opportunity."

On Thursday night, December 9, 1982, the telephone rang in a colleague's office. My appeal was successful. The Committee said that given the "totality of the circumstances," it would be a manifest injustice" if they did not license me.

I telephoned Mom and Dad in Ohio and then, Carole and Neil. Then I called John, my attorney. I was crying when he answered the phone. He knew who it was. He said, "Congratulations, counselor. You've just won your first case."

Over the next three years, I won other cases — quite a few. Eighty-five per cent of all criminal appeals that I responded to were upheld by the Utah Supreme Court. Besides writing briefs, I had the heady experience of presenting "oral arguments" on thirty cases.

Responding to questions from five Supreme Court justices was as exhilarating as it was intimidating. But the pressures and demands of a criminal appellate attorney are harsh. Predictably, I burned out.

I was exposed to most, if not all, issues that criminal defendants raised on appeal. I grew tired of reading transcript after transcript of such heinous acts as rape, child abuse and murder. What convinced me that a reassignment was necessary was when a Supreme Court insider told me that I was highly respected by the justices and that they considered me a talented advocate. With that endorsement, I believed it was time to change the scenery. I knew if the justices saw me more frequently in ensuing years, the law of diminishing returns would catch up with me.

I was reassigned by the Attorney General to represent the Utah Division of Occupational and Professional Licensing. This Division regulated over thirty professions in Utah, ranging from physicians to accountants to massage therapists. I prosecuted professionals for unethical conduct and unlawful practices, including sexual misconduct, substance abuse or fraudulent over billing of services.

Ironically, I was cross-examining physicians and nurses, the types of professionals who had always considered me "just another patient" during my hospital stays. It was my responsibility to protect not only the high standards of these professions but also the interests and safety of their patients.

Because of this experience, I wanted to raise the level of professionalism within the Bar. I knew that if other professionals were being disciplined because of alcohol and substance abuse, then certainly lawyers were not immune from these challenges. I became a member of the Utah Bar's "Lawyers Helping Lawyers" Committee which assisted and supported attorneys impaired as a result of alcoholism, substance abuse, or clinical depression.

I informed the Chairman of the Bar Committee that, unlike some of the attorneys on the Committee, I was not "recovering" from substance abuse nor had I ever been diagnosed with long-term depression. I told him that because of my physical disability I believed I could empathize with and encourage those who were addressing their disabilities. I said, "Just because we can't see them doesn't mean that they are any less formidable. Alcoholism, mental illness and substance abuse are invisible disabilities but they are every bit as daunting and overwhelming as my muscle disease has been in my life. Every day brings both challenge and hope that we can contribute to our profession and enjoy life, notwithstanding our weaknesses. I think I have something to offer this Committee."

A year after that conversation, I was appointed Chairman of the Lawyers Helping Lawyers Committee. At least two or three times a month I received a call from the Office of Bar counsel, a concerned judge or a distraught spouse regarding an attorney whose life was out of control and whose clients were being neglected, ignored or incompetently served. I would inform the attorney that concerns had been raised about problems that might be impeding his or her ability to practice. Usually, their response would be a vehement denial.

I would invite them to my office to discuss the matter further and tell them that their communications with me and the Committee were confidential and protected by the attorney-client privilege. I reassured them that I was chiefly concerned with their welfare and that if they did have a problem we had a network of assistance to help them regain control of their lives and resume a responsible and manageable practice.

Many times at these meetings, I would invite a psychologist or social worker to conduct an "intervention," to confront the person about his or her alcoholism or substance abuse and to recommend that he or she seek professional help.

It was so gratifying whenever we penetrated the attorney's denial and watched him or her assume responsibility for their behavior. Increasing numbers of bar associations throughout the country are educating their members that over half of all attorneys disciplined for unprofessional or unethical behavior stems from substance abuse. Nothing made me happier than to see a colleague start down the road towards recovery, one day at a time.

Chapter 26

Little did I know that my experience with the Lawyers Helping Lawyers Committee would prepare me to intervene in the life of the person most important to me — my mother. When my parents returned from a dream vacation to China and Japan in November 1985, Mom appeared irritable and forgetful. She was fatigued and her attention span seemed shorter. We all assumed she was depressed.

Throughout her life, she had bouts of depression, which would not incapacitate her, but did lower her energy levels and increase her emotions. She would always pull herself out of her "funk," as she referred to it, but this time the depression did not disappear in a couple of days.

I attributed this latest mood swing to the fact that she had immersed herself in genealogy — the study of one's ancestors. She had devoted the last three years of her life to obtaining as much information as possible about the Lazich and Mikita families. Mom and Dad made several trips to Yugoslavia so she could trace her roots and obtain oral histories from relatives living behind the Iron Curtain. She was enthralled with every aspect of her research.

But her work had loosened childhood memories that she had suppressed for too long. While exploring her ancestral history, Mom could not stop the dark memories of her own.

When I would telephone Dad wondering how she was doing, he, too, said little more than, "Oh, Mommy is thinking a lot about when she was a little girl, Stef. She'll be okay, though."

Dad was alluding to my grandparents' tumultuous relationship. The simple fact that my grandmother proudly told us that she never loved my grandfather was enough to explain the dysfunction and confusion that Mom was now struggling to reconcile.

I suggested that Dad take her to a psychologist to help her resolve the conflicts. I knew that he was not a proponent of psychotherapy. He came from the old school of medicine and the era that viewed such treatment with skepticism.

He'd say, "Well, we'll see. I just think I need to get her out of here for a while and away from her parents. Once we get her out to Palm Springs, after Carole has her baby in January, I think Mommy is going to feel a lot better. Keep calling to tell her what you're doing. That always makes her feel better." I knew it would take more than the sun and the desert to restore Mom's deteriorating mental health.

My worries escalated when she arrived in Salt Lake City in January 1986 for the birth of Carole and Neil's second child. After picking Mom up at the airport, Carole telephoned me at the office. She was alarmed. "Stevie, Mommy doesn't look well. She's so overweight and her face is misshapen. It takes her so much energy to walk. She's acting like she's eighty years old. When we got home, all she wanted to do was sit on the couch. Stevie, that's not Mom. You know, any other time, she immediately starts cleaning or cooking something. She even doesn't seem as interested in Jennifer, (Carole's three-year-old daughter). Stevie, I'm really worried about her."

I said, "Well, I'll talk to her and see how she's doing. Don't worry about her. Just conserve your strength. I'll talk to her about counseling, when she goes home or maybe she can start it in Palm Springs."

If anything was to awaken Mom from her lethargy and melancholy, I thought it would be the birth of her newest granddaughter, Caitlin Kingsmill York. Amazingly, it didn't.

When Carole returned home from the hospital, Mom was of little or no help. Even her emotional reaction to the new baby was unusually restrained, almost indifferent.

The next day, Carole called me in the morning, "Stevie, I'm worried. I asked Mom to be here at my house at 8:30 to help me with Jennifer and the baby. That was three hours ago! I'm worried that something has happened to her."

I said, "Don't worry, I'll get in touch with her. Maybe she's fallen asleep at my place. I'll call there." There was no answer. I wasn't going to panic and knew there had to be a logical explanation for Mom's delay.

The Third Opinion

Finally, at 1:00 p.m., Mom arrived at Carole's. She was apathetic about being so late. She said that she had taken her time getting ready and had gone shopping. That was bizarre.

I asked Carole to put her on the telephone. I said, "Mommy, what is going on? Carole and I have been worried sick. Where have you been? Mommy, Carole needs your help. That's why you're here. You told her at eight o'clock, you were on your way. What have you been doing?"

Mom didn't sound the least apologetic. Her response was so out of character. She said only, "Well, I'm here now. I'll help her."

She was numb to my questions and criticism. My words had no effect on her. Carole and I were baffled. Mom had become a stranger.

The next day, Mom telephoned Dad and asked him to come to Utah to take her back to Steubenville. She wanted to go home. Dad said, "No, honey, why don't you stay there and help Carole and the baby."

Mom remained determined, "No, I want to go home."

None of this was making any sense. Nothing came before her children or grandchildren. I thought Mom must really be depressed.

The day before Dad arrived to escort her home, another frightening event occurred. Three-year-old Jennifer wanted to go to a nearby strip mall to buy a gold fish. Mom volunteered to take her. On their return trip to Carole's house, Mom told Jennifer that she couldn't remember what street they needed to take to get home. Jennifer directed her grandmother to their home and then innocently reported to Carole that she and Grammy had gotten lost. She had to tell Grammy how to drive back.

A week after she returned home, Mom improved slightly. She was more animated and less tired. She and Dad went to New Orleans for the American College of Surgeons annual convention.

Dad soon realized that they should not have gone. The first afternoon, Mom called for his help; she didn't have the strength to stand up in the bath tub. The next day Mom left their hotel room at 3:00 p.m. to shop. Dad reminded her that they had dinner reservations at 7:30 p.m. Mom returned at midnight! She was unable to tell Dad where she had been and what she had done. She simply had lost track of the time. Dad was exasperated. They left New Orleans the next afternoon.

Two weeks later they were planning a month-long vacation in

Palm Springs, California. For the last five years, they had spent a month "in the desert," as Mom affectionately referred to it. She loved everything about it — the sun, the heat, the red rocks and the flora. Each of us would join them for a few days. It was a glorious reminder of our best and most memorable times as a family.

Dad was still optimistic that they could make their annual sojourn, despite Mom's depression. Three days before their departure, I telephoned home to check on her. Finally, after the twentieth ring, Mom answered. Her voice sounded feeble and flat. "Hello?" she said.

"Mom, are you okay?" I asked.

"Yeah, I'm okay."

I wasn't convinced. "Mom, what are you doing? Why did you take so long to answer the phone?"

She said, simply, "I've been sleeping."

I said, "Mom it's 12:30 in the afternoon. Why are you sleeping?"

She said, "I'm just so tired. I guess I've got to start packing for Palm Springs. We're leaving tomorrow."

I said, "Mom, you're not leaving tomorrow."

"We're not?" she asked.

"No!"

She then asked, "What day is it?"

I answered, "Mom, it's Wednesday. You don't know what day it is? Mom, are you really that depressed?"

She said, "I guess so."

Trembling, I said, "Mom, I'm going to call Dad. You go back to bed and rest. I'll talk to you tonight."

In a monotone, she just said, "Okay." She was so lifeless.

I was crying and shaking as I dialed Dad's office number. I told his secretary, Patty, that I needed to talk to him immediately. She said he was visiting with a patient, but that she would interrupt him. As soon as he picked up the phone I said, "Dad, something is terribly wrong with Mom. I just called her, Dad. The phone rang forever and when she picked it up she said she had been sleeping. She didn't know what time it was. Dad, she didn't even know what day it is. She thought it was Friday and you were leaving for Palm Springs tomorrow. Please, Dad, call a psychiatrist and get her some help."

Dad said, "Okay, Stef. I'll cancel the trip to Palm Springs and take her to Pittsburgh to see a psychiatrist."

I said, "Thanks, Dad. I'm really worried about her."

The Third Opinion

The next day, Dad took her to Pittsburgh. He was no longer in denial about Mom's condition. He was decisive. He told me to call that night so he could report what the psychiatrist said.

What the psychiatrist said was horrifying.

Dad said, "Stef, Mommy is severely depressed. She even told the doctor that she has contemplated committing suicide. He wants to hospitalize her on Monday. They're waiting for a bed to open up."

"Dad, what's caused this?"

Dad replied, "I don't know. He needs to observe her longer."

"Dad, is she suicidal, now?"

He said, "I don't think so. But I'll watch her. Billy is bringing his girls over this weekend. That might make her feel better."

I said, "Dad, where is she now?"

Dad said, "She's been sleeping ever since we got home."

I started crying. "Dad, tell her I love her and she's got to fight this and not give up. Make sure there's someone there to watch her, Dad, when you go to the hospital in the morning."

Dad said, "I've already called Helen (our longtime housekeeper) and she'll be here at eight o'clock to watch her."

"Dad, I'll call you tomorrow."

When I hung up the phone, I was engulfed by the terrible realization that my mother — my anchor and life force — had actually contemplated killing herself. That's how little life meant to her at the moment, I thought. That's how ill she was.

My grief and terror drew me to a collage of family photographs on my bedroom wall. I stared at one of my favorites. It showed Mom and Dad in their bathing suits, leaning over my wheelchair. We were at Rehobeth Beach in Delaware. It was July 4, 1980. She looked so beautiful, happy and alive. And there was her smile that came so naturally. The smile that always told me how much she loved me had now been replaced by a brooding frown, evidence of a disturbed mind, I felt.

While I looked at the photograph, I imagined her trying to escape her internal hell. I feared what would happen to her between Friday and Monday morning when she would go to the psychiatric hospital. One after another, I conjured ways in which she could kill herself. There were never any guns in our house, but the kitchen had a variety of knives, and if no one were watching....

Dad said Mom had no energy. Once she was upstairs in their bedroom, he was certain she would not be wandering the halls and floors of our home. Nevertheless, I feared the worst. She could simply open a window in their bedroom and jump from the second story or find some pills in the medicine cabinet.

My mind was racing. It was so unreal. After calculating her suicide options, I was struck with an indelible impression: Mom was never going to be the same. I tried purging that thought from my mind. But I couldn't. I didn't know what the future would hold. I only knew that Mom was never going to fully recover.

I also felt that our relationship would change. Our roles would reverse. I would need to be the strong one. I would have to lift her spirits. I didn't want to do it, but I had no other choice. That night I began mourning the loss of my mother.

However, I did need to do all I could to prevent her from committing suicide. I telephoned Billy in Cincinnati and told him to definitely go home for the weekend, but not to take his daughters, Natalie and Jacqueline. He needed to be there completely for Mom and to watch her constantly.

The next morning, I briefed our housekeeper, Helen, who Mom called "my best friend." I asked Helen to protect Mom and to check in on her as frequently as possible, until Dad returned from the hospital.

I talked to Mom only a couple of times that weekend. She spoke in a weak monotone. I said essentially the same thing both times. "Mommy, I love you. Life is worth living. You need to fight, Mom. Don't give up. You're going to be okay. I love you and I'm praying for you."

I wasn't sure that she even heard me. My words were bouncing off her. I felt helpless.

Monday morning came and she was still alive. She had made it through the weekend.

Chapter 27

I thought Mom merely needed some intense counseling and drug therapy. Dad reported that she was not improving. She was becoming incoherent. She lost a sense of time and place. She was disoriented.

When I talked to her on the telephone each day, I prayed that I would hear a stronger, more determined voice. I had to identify myself by name. Even then, I wasn't sure she knew who she was talking to.

She told me that Dad hadn't come to visit her for a while when, in fact, he was practically living at her bedside. When she talked of her children, she referred to us as adolescents. One day she even told Dad that she had seen me in another hospital room.

When I spoke to her, I asked question after question. She ignored most of them. She never elaborated. Just one word responses. "Yeah." "No." "Okay." I exhorted her to not give up — as she had told me during my hospitalizations. Most of our conversations were really nothing more than monologues. I tried everything from her own repertoire to motivate her.

Dad said I wasn't the only one not getting through. She wasn't participating during her group therapy sessions. She preferred sleeping. When she was awake, she appeared agitated.

Toward the end of the first week, I was facing another crisis — kidney stones. Since October 1981 I had endured three bouts of kidney stones. Twice I required surgery, because I was unable to pass them. Each time I experienced that unrelenting pain that has been compared by some to contractions in childbirth. The doctors attributed my susceptibility to producing stones to dehydration and my inability to empty my bladder fully.

I couldn't believe the poor timing. Mom had only been hospitalized once during my life and that for a hysterectomy. Now, she was 2,000 miles away in a psychiatric hospital. I felt so frightened. I had never been hospitalized without her. Dad said Mom's doctor asked that we not tell her where I was or what I was going through so as not to send her into a tailspin.

My kidney stones were not moving down the urethra. Surgery was necessary.

Mom was getting steadily worse. She had become incontinent. Dad said that after ten days of doing nothing for her, the doctors finally scheduled a CAT scan.

The night before my surgery, Dad telephoned my hospital room. Carole answered the phone. Her first words were "Dear God, no!" She looked up from the phone with utter despair. "Stevie, Mommy has a brain tumor! She only has six weeks to live!"

Dad was in shock. He never sounded so sad and vulnerable.

My worst nightmare had come true. Mom was dying of cancer! Brain cancer! She only had six weeks! How could this happen? How could she die before me? I never imagined that ever occurring. It was not part of my plan. I thought that she would always be there for me. One thing I counted on was that I would never outlive her. Dad had always joked she would probably live until she was 100. Mom's father was 90 and still driving his car. She had just turned sixty. This couldn't be happening.

I was being asked to survive this surgery without her by my side. Soon, I would be required to live without her. I wasn't sure I was strong enough to do either.

We asked Dad whether Mom knew she was dying. He said she didn't. We asked whether he was going to tell her. He said the doctors saw no reason for it. Even assuming that she might comprehend what they were saying, they feared it would only hasten her death. Dad asked whether I needed him to come out for the surgery.

I said, "No, Dad. Mom needs you more. Carole is here and she'll take care of me."

Carole and I would travel through this new experience together. I wasn't alone and neither was she. At least we had each other. We didn't know how we would get through the next few days without

The Third Opinion

Mom, just that we had to.

Predictably, my body had a violent reaction to the anesthetic after kidney surgery. I couldn't stop vomiting. I was in terrible pain. How I wished Mom was there to hold my hand and comfort me!

In less than a day, I was having gruesome dreams and saying things that made no sense. I was in delirium. I had been over medicated. The nurses had not monitored my intake and output of fluids. Consequently, my body was retaining too much pain medication.

I repeatedly shook my head in order to expunge the horrible images that dominated my dreams every time I closed my eyes.

Carole and Neil were furious at the ineptness of the staff that caused this to happen. I had warned them prior to surgery how sensitive my body was to narcotics.

When I stabilized the following day, I telephoned Mom. I was surprised that she sounded better. She told me I didn't sound very well. I lied and said, "Well, Mom, I'm just really working hard. I think I'm a little tired and my throat is scratchy. I'm fine. Don't worry, Mom. I miss you and love you. I'll see you soon."

I meant it. I had to see her before she died. I had to get better and get stronger as soon as possible. She was running out of time and she needed me.

In April, two weeks after surgery, I was ready to travel home to see her. My hospitalization and recovery were still secrets. That was so difficult and painful. I never kept anything from her. But I was willing to do anything to keep her with us longer, even if that required that I couldn't tell her the truth about her or me.

I hoped that my visit would somehow produce a miracle. I prayed that my love was powerful enough to heal her and cause the large tumor in the front of her brain to disappear.

I just needed her too much. She couldn't be dying!

When I was wheeled into the house, it felt different. Mom had always been the hub of activity. Her spirit permeated the home. Now that spirit was gone. She wasn't there to greet me. Dad said she was napping before dinner.

Home wasn't home anymore. Mom was sick, dying of a brain tumor. Her health and her home had changed.

Dad tried to be cheerful and upbeat. But he couldn't conceal his preoccupation. Again, he was the victim of a cruel fate. He was told when I was eighteen months old that I only had six months to live.

Now he was being told that Mom only had six weeks. He could only watch and wait to see whether death would pass over her as it had me.

I could tell that he was in much more pain than Mom, both physically and emotionally. He knew too much about medicine to believe that she had a good chance of surviving the tumor. Yet, he was a fighter and was not going to give up.

Every night he would sit in his familiar chair in the family room and read his daily dose of five newspapers. Every twenty minutes he would sprint up the winding staircase to their bedroom when Mom needed something. He spoke to her in such sweet, solicitous tones. No matter how many times she called, he never seemed to mind. He cut back his surgery schedule. He was getting very little sleep and didn't need the added worry of having to be as focused on his patients' needs. For now, at least, he only had one patient to care for.

I recalled how many times he had told us that the greatest gift that a father can give his children is the knowledge that he loves their mother. Now with every "Okay, babe" or "I'm coming, honey," or "I'll be downstairs if you need me, Doll," I knew she, too, was his greatest gift.

When I saw her that evening, it wasn't nearly as frightening as I had feared. She looked weak, unfocused and bloated. Dad said her weight gain was caused by the cortisone that was prescribed to reduce the tumor's growth.

I was afraid that she would notice that my left leg was twice its size because of fluid build-up as a result of my recent kidney surgery. But she didn't. She initiated no conversation. She seemed to be operating on pure, maternal instinct. She was dazed and completely unaware that she had a brain tumor and was dying.

Dad reassured me she was in no pain and that because of the tumor's placement, Mom was unable to grasp her present or her future with any certainty. In fact, the only time that she was confronted with the awful truth that she had brain cancer by a hospice worker, she indignantly declared, "I don't have cancer. Get out of my house!"

As a last resort, Dad believed that she should undergo radiation therapy. Mom's physicians said a benign lymphoma would respond favorably to the treatments, but there was only a 1 in 2,000 chance of that happening. Dad said radiation was worth a try, regardless of their skepticism.

The Third Opinion

Besides being skeptical about radiation, I feared that Mom would suffer from the treatment. I couldn't bear the thought of having her lie inside a machine and not realize the meaning of it all. I didn't want her to be confused or traumatized by the experience. I also dreaded the fact that she would lose her hair.

How could Mom be sick? I was good at being the hospital patient. I understood the rugged terrain of hospitals, their hazards and dangers. Mom didn't. She shared so many of my experiences, but she was distanced from them because of her health.

She had been through enough with me, I thought. She didn't deserve this awful fate, to be alone, inside a machine, while we hoped and prayed for a miracle.

The radiation reduced some of the swelling around the tumor. Mom became more lucid. At least she knew who I was and where she was.

Over the next several months, I could not always control my tears or my fears during our telephone visits. Sometimes Mom would ask me, "I feel like you want to tell me something." Is there something the matter, Luddel (her way of saying lover)?"

I strained to compose myself so as not to reveal the truth that she was dying and we would be separated until my death.

I'd say, "I don't know, Mom. I just get scared sometimes. I wish you didn't have to go through this. I don't want you to be afraid of the future."

She would say, "Oh, I'm not afraid, Doll. I don't want you to be afraid. How can I be afraid with you as an example? Remember, I'm the mother of a brave little boy who was asked to endure a lot more at a much earlier age than I am. With your example of courage, how can I do anything less?"

"Mom you've got to keep on fighting."

"Oh, don't worry, you taught me how to fight. Now, don't you worry about me. You and I have been through a lot worse things than this."

I'd hang up the phone and weep. This was absolutely the worst thing that had ever happened to me! I was going to lose the greatest part of me, and only one of us knew it.

Chapter 28

During that summer, Mom's condition remained largely unchanged. Judy, pregnant with her first child, postponed her dance commitments in Chicago to care for Mom during the radiation treatments. Dad said there was still that slight chance the tumor would disappear.

On August 29, Mom was given another CAT SCAN. I called Dad that night for the results. I was in Snowbird, Utah, spending a couple of days with friends at one of Utah's all-season resorts.

Dad's voice sounded lighter than it had for nine months.

He said, "Hi, Stef. Mommy had the CAT-SCAN today. The tumor is gone! The doctors couldn't believe it. But I looked at it. There's nothing there!"

"What's that mean, Dad?"

"Well, I guess that it was a lymphoma that they had said it had a 1 in 2,000 chance of it being."

I couldn't believe what I was hearing. "Does this mean she's in remission, Dad?" He wasn't sure. He obviously didn't want to get into the details. That tempered some of my jubilation.

I never thought this good news would last. I couldn't forget that feeling that I had on the night that Mom had gone to the psychiatrist. She would never be the same. I knew my guarded reaction disappointed Dad.

Dad remarked, "As your cousin, Connie Rothermel, said a couple of months ago, 'If anyone is deserving of a miracle, it's your Mom.' Here, let me put Mommy on!"

The Third Opinion

I said, "Mom, this is great news. Our prayers have been answered."

She said, "I know, isn't it wonderful. We're so happy and blessed." But she seemed to be reading from a script. The tumor, whatever type it was, had played havoc with her emotions. She still didn't sound like herself and that stoked my suspicions that her march towards death had only been delayed, not cancelled. I knew the tumor would return.

As the holidays approached, Mom's health declined. Mom had been given only a temporary reprieve. This would be our last Christmas with her.

The tumor returned. There was nothing more that could be done for her. Miraculously, she was still not in any pain. Sadly, all any of us could do was prepare for the inevitable — Mom was going to die.

Christmas was tense and sorrowful. Everything we did, from decorating the tree, to exchanging presents, to taking a formal family photograph, to having Christmas dinner were grim reminders that we were doing it all for the last time. Everyone tried to put the happiest spin possible on every family ritual and tradition. But it felt so pointless. We were pretending that everything was fine, when, in fact, everything wasn't.

It was doubly painful to accept Mom's pending death, when her damaged brain prevented her from even understanding it. Even when reading her own medical chart documenting her terminal condition, Mom stated: "They continue saying I have cancer. They don't know what they're talking about, I don't have cancer."

The medical explanation for her blanket denial of her condition was a metastatic tumor inside her brain. But there was another reason that explained her denial. It was her essence to transcend medical predictions. She began in 1958 when the NIH physicians told her that I had no chance, no hope and no future. After thirty years of listening to and then defying one prognosis after another, Mom was just fighting the same fight. But this time she was the patient. One thing remained a constant — her will, her way.

In February, Dad took Mom to Chicago so a neurosurgeon could evaluate her tumor. The night before the surgery, a chest x-ray disclosed more tragic news — there was a cancerous tumor on one of Mom's ribs. It was inoperable. That made the brain surgery the next day an exercise in futility. Not surprisingly, the surgeon found nothing, but burned and scarred tissue, when he opened her skull. The radiation had done its damage and now the tumor on the rib would take care of the rest.

Nevertheless, Dad thought they should go one final time to the desert. I met them in Palm Springs in April 1987. Mom looked and acted like she was dying.

She was like an infant. Her days were spent eating and sleeping. We practically ate all of our meals at the condominium. A couple of times we ventured out, but it was obvious that Mom was in no condition to enjoy herself.

One afternoon, my attendant and I went to the Dinah Shore Open at the Rancho Mirage Country Club. Dad said that he and Mom would meet us there. As we walked towards the clubhouse, Mom and Dad were seated near the eighteenth green. Mom looked very uncomfortable and tired; she needed a nap.

After my attendant lifted me in the front seat of the car, he folded my wheelchair and placed it into the trunk. He left to help Dad to escort Mom back to the car. Every step she took required so much effort. At one point, one of her knees buckled. She couldn't take another step.

Dad ran back to the car and opened the trunk to get the wheelchair. To witness my mother having to sit in my wheelchair was gut-wrenching. I felt the senseless horror of her illness and the pitiful state of her existence.

The next day I had to return to Utah. I knew it would probably be the last time that I would ever see her alive. It was unbearable having to say goodbye.

When I was wheeled into her bedroom, she asked Dad to sit her on the edge of the bed. I clasped her hand and said, "I don't want to leave you, Mommy. I just want to sit here and hold your hand and take care of you. I love you so much."

She said, "Don't worry about me. I love you, but you have to leave and become that man that we always talked about you becoming when you were a little boy. Don't be afraid. I'm not afraid."

Although we talked by telephone after that, that was the last coherent, meaningful dialogue we had.

She had very little left. I traveled to Ohio in July, but didn't talk to her. She was sleeping most of the day. She was awake long enough to go to the bathroom and eat a little something. By the first week in

The Third Opinion

September, it only became a matter of days. By the second weekend, she lapsed into a coma. On Saturday, September 12, Dad telephoned Carole and me and told us that this was the end. Mom's breathing was labored and her kidneys were not functioning. I made plans to leave on Monday, September 14.

On Sunday, I attended a friend's wedding reception.

When I returned from the reception, I called Mom's room. It was 8:00 p.m. in Ohio. Judy answered and said Mom was fading. I told her to place the telephone next to Mom's ear. When Judy had placed it, I could hear Mom's heavy, slow breaths.

I said, "Mommy, this is Stevie." Immediately, her breathing changed. It was stronger, faster. She knew who I was! She was still fighting.

I said, "Mommy, I don't want you to keep fighting. It's time for you to go home and live with Heavenly Father. Don't stay alive for me. I don't want you to worry about me, Mom. Carole will look after me and take care of me. It's time Mom for you to go home to heaven. Just let go. I love you, Mommy, and will miss you so much. But I will see you soon..I love you."

Judy took the phone away. She said she knew that Mom heard and understood my final plea.

As I boarded the plane the next morning, I had only one wish — to see her one last time, for one final embrace, one farewell kiss, and one last glimpse of her, my wingless angel. Cancer had already captured her brain, but I stubbornly refused to concede, to surrender.

I could not conceive of living without her, not to mention, trying to fulfill our dreams alone.

Her life was indistinguishable. Her life was indispensable. Her life was inseparable from mine. How could she leave me behind? How could I go on? She was my light through the darkness, my calm through the storms, my salve for every wound.

Now, she would be gone. We had so much left to do. She was my fuel and my fire and they were being extinguished. I just wanted to see her before she left me.

As the plane took off from Salt Lake City, I felt drowsy and began nodding off, despite my fear of flying.

It was a beautiful pristine morning as we flew over the Rocky Mountains of Wyoming. Twice, I was startled from my slumber by a blinding light, which I erroneously concluded emanated from outside the windows of the aircraft. But a third time, the shaft of lightening returned, and I unmistakably heard a voice. It said, "Stevie."

It was a happy voice. It was a healthy voice. It was a familiar voice. It was Mom's voice.

When the plane landed in Pittsburgh later that afternoon, my brother, Billy, boarded the plane and I asked, "Did I make it in time?"

Billy's moistened eyes answered me before he spoke, "No, Stef, Mommy died this morning."

I asked him, "What time did she die?"

Billy said, "At 11:30 a.m."

I thought back to the scene on the plane, hours before, when I had seen that brilliant light and heard her precious voice. That was 9:30 a.m. Mountain Daylight Time!

Mothers never truly die; they never say goodbye. Their influence, legacy and spirit remain closer than we think, to nurture and remind us who we are and what we can become, if we do not become embittered. After that experience, I knew I had not been abandoned. I knew Mom had not forgotten how much I loved and needed her.

At Mom's funeral three days later, her four children were the only speakers. We were convinced that's what she wanted. I told Billy, Carole, and Judy, as we gathered for a family prayer, prior to leaving for the church, "This is our opportunity, our only opportunity, to tell Mom's family and friends how truly great and powerful she was. There will be plenty of time for us to grieve her. Today, we must honor and celebrate her."

When it was my turn, I told the cramped congregation that I desired them to "understand and behold the beauty, elegance, dignity and sheer majesty of my life's greatest blessing — my mother." I said, "Rather than lament the fact that she could not teach me how to walk and to run, instead she taught me how to dream without pitying and how to pray without kneeling. So many times it was her smile that kept me going, her faith that kept me believing and her love that kept me living."

"Currently, I am in that period of darkness called grief and mourning, with the dawn of relief not immediately identifiable. I am not hopelessly or bitterly sitting in the dark, imprisoned by loneliness, fear or a sense of injustice."

Alluding to my experience on the plane, I explained, "She is not asleep, but very much alive. . . . Her separation from us is as temporary

The Third Opinion

and brief as her love for us is permanent and eternal. We have not been abandoned, forgotten or forsaken. . . . Her priority will not suddenly change. Mom will continue doing what she did best — loving her husband and children."

"As she did every evening after tucking me into bed and before saying good night, Mom has again covered me with her eternal blanket of love and switched on the night light near the door to comfort me during her absence."

"When the distraught physicians predicted that I would tarry no longer than two years, they had obviously overlooked the angelic ministrant, who held me so fervently and securely in her arms and quietly, but stubbornly, refused to obey their prognosis of resigned defeat."

"These are the night lights which Mom has given me which emblazon my room and pierce my soul with a truth and a love that transcend even the cruelest and most cancerous of crucibles. Those lights will protect, console and nurture me during this night when we must be apart."

"Mom, it's not too dark. I'm not afraid anymore. See you in the morning. I love you, Mom!"

Chapter 29

In spite of my perspective on the day that we buried her, I was lost following my return to Utah. I really had no plans, no ambitions, no dreams. They seemed to disappear with Mom's body.

Life without her wasn't fun anymore. I didn't have either the energy or the desire to start over. My life was unraveling.

I dreaded having to face what would have been her sixty-second birthday without her, October 23. I was recruiting new attendants. After two days of interviewing over twenty applicants, I hired the best candidates.

However, there was one interview left. I planned on making it as short as possible since I had already filled the positions. I was tired of asking questions and describing the job. I was thinking a lot about Mom, too. But the last interviewee needed a job. When Diane Cunningham walked into my office, I started smiling, healing and dreaming again.

I created a job for her, not because I needed her help, but because I needed a friend and confidant.

We only talked ten minutes. I knew Diane had not come into my life by accident. She reignited my fire that had been extinguished by Mom's death.

When she left my office, I knew Mom had remembered me on her birthday and given me the gift of Diane. She even looked angelic with her naturally blonde hair and sleepy blue eyes. I didn't care that my new guardian angel chain-smoked Marlboros.

But Diane, unfortunately, never met Mom and she hadn't known me prior to Mom's illness and death. She couldn't really measure my progress without knowing my past. Although my spirit was restored, I lacked my intense focus and drive. It was time for another reminder of who I was and where I had come from.

On the weekend before my thirty-second birthday, Martha Mueller, my close friend from Duke, came to visit. She unknowingly inspired me. One evening before leaving for dinner, Martha and I were talking about her latest romantic interest. In describing her new boyfriend, Martha said, "But Steve, he's not like you and me; he doesn't have that killer instinct." My entire body tingled.

I asked Martha what she meant. "Oh, you know exactly what I mean." I did. I had just forgotten it since the day Mom died. Tears filled my eyes and tenacity returned to my heart.

My fight was back. I was still Mom's son. I couldn't stop living. I had to keep striving to achieve both my dreams and hers. They were still our dreams. It was time to move on. I had felt sorry for myself for long enough.

I knew what I needed to do and what Mom wanted me to do. I knew the plan. I had no doubt that I could accomplish the work that she left me to do. There was nothing that she needed to add to the plan. I knew how she felt about me, and she knew precisely what she meant to me. There was nothing else to say. We had said it all.

Anything else would have been merely a review of something we had already discussed and agreed to do. She would always be with me. If she had lived, the plan would not have changed. She had given me everything I needed.

Martha reminded me that I did have the fight and the faith to take my first steps without holding Mom's hand. It was time to figuratively stand on my own two feet and upon the foundation that we had built. It didn't take long for me to hit my stride.

In the spring of 1989, I was informed that I had been named "Utah's Outstanding Young Lawyer of the Year." I received the award at the Utah Bar Association's Annual Convention, which was held that year in Sun Valley, Idaho, a place that quickly became my favorite vacation spot. I was honored for my excellence in and service to the legal profession, particularly, in light of my involvement with the Lawyers Helping Lawyers Committee.

In 1990, I was appointed as the only disabled member of the Salt Lake City Winter Olympic Committee after I expressed my desire to make the Salt Lake Olympic Games in 2002 the most accessible games in history for anyone with a disability.

In July 1990, President Bush signed into law the Americans with Disabilities Act or "ADA." The ADA extended civil rights protections and guarantees to some forty-nine million Americans with disabilities. President Bush called it the "Emancipation Proclamation" for disabled Americans.

This new federal law covers five major aspects of American life: employment, state and local government services, public accommodations (i.e., private businesses engaged in commerce), public transportation and telecommunications.

I was ecstatic about the passage of the ADA. I knew it would take time for businesses and employers to comply with the new requirements. What I didn't expect was that I would become known as one of the nation's experts on the Americans with Disabilities Act.

In the fall of 1991, Mary Anne Wood, a law professor at BYU, invited me to participate in a conference that her law firm was sponsoring for employers in Salt Lake City. I told Mary Anne I felt inadequate to talk about a law that I knew very little about. Mary Anne said she would furnish me a copy of both the law and its regulations.

There were at least fifty businesses represented at the conference. Mary Anne said that of all the presenters. I was the most popular and had received the highest rating from the attendees. Mary Anne said, "Not only do you understand the technical requirements of the ADA, but your personal anecdotes put a human face on the law that encourages many leery businesses to open their doors to Americans with disabilities."

Many national associations and businesses approached me to lecture about this new civil rights law.

From the American Association of Architects to the United States Army, to the American Bar Association, my message about the ADA was essentially the same.

I explained, "The Americans with Disabilities Act is about more than ramps, extra-wide doorways, elevators and special parking spaces. It's about real people, with real feelings, real dreams and real nightmares. They are real people like you and me.

"Just because they may talk differently, walk differently, speak differently, hear differently, see differently or think differently does not mean that they are any less deserving of the protections of American law and pleasures of American life."

The Third Opinion

"In 1964, Congress passed the Civil Rights Act to end religious, race, gender and ethnic discrimination. There was no mention of the word "handicapped" or "disabled" in that law. Not until 26 years later did Congress extend those protections to the single largest minority in our country, Americans with disabilities."

"The ADA is about the fundamental principles of our democratic republic — liberty, equality and fairness. It is not an "us" versus "them" proposition. We are not inferior Americans or children of a lesser god."

"I believe all of us are Americans with disabilities. Each of us has strengths, talents, skills and abilities — things that we are good at and excel in. But each of us has weaknesses, shortcomings, deficiencies and disabilities. We should all be evaluated and accepted on the basis of our abilities, not discriminated against because of our disabilities."

I tell my audiences of an interview that I had with Lois Collins, a reporter for Salt Lake City's newspaper, *The Deseret News*, on the date the ADA became effective — January 26, 1992. Lois inquired, "Steve, does the ADA have any real impact on you, personally? After all, you've lived the balance of your life and achieved great things from your wheelchair without the ADA. Does this new law mean anything to you?"

Not until Lois posed that question, did I realize that I had spent the last ten years as an Assistant Attorney General interpreting, arguing and enforcing laws that were significant to other citizens' lives, but not mine.

Before the passage of the ADA, there was never a law that was relevant to my life, both my ambitions and frustrations. There was never a law that understood and acknowledged me.

I told Lois that this new law reminded me of our first family vacation to Washington, D.C., when I was five years old. Our first stop was the Lincoln Memorial. What separated Mr. Lincoln and me were several levels of steps. It was 1960.

There was no elevator to help me reach the Memorial, so Dad gathered me in his arms and carried me to the top. But by the time that we had reached the summit, I felt different from the other tourists who were standing in our midst. Not only was I worried about all the energy it took Dad to hold me, but also I felt as if I didn't belong there because I couldn't walk like everyone else. I wasn't really welcome.

Twenty years after that experience, I was back in Washington clerking for the Senate Judiciary Committee. On a blistering Friday afternoon in July, I decided to bump off work early. Orrin Hatch had left the office that morning to return to Utah. I wanted to check in on Mr. Lincoln.

This time the experience was altogether different. Dad wasn't there to lift me up those many stairs. But in the intervening twenty years, an elevator was installed.

When I reached the top, I sat right in front of him. I felt like I had been invited. I felt like I belonged. I felt like that was as much my memorial as it was anyone else's that day. I felt like an American.

It was absolutely exhilarating, emancipating and empowering. That is what the Americans with Disabilities Act means to me. I think President Lincoln would approve of the ADA.

Later in 1992, I was informed that I had been nominated for a national award because of my disability rights advocacy and professional accomplishments. It was known as the National Personal Achievement Award and it was sponsored by the Muscular Dystrophy Association. I knew that MDA was synonymous with the name and icon, Jerry Lewis.

I had always admired Jerry Lewis, not just because he is a comic genius, but also for his commitment to finding a cure for forty neuromuscular diseases. When I was ten years old, I told Mom, while we watched the annual Labor Day Telethon, "One day I'd like to meet Jerry Lewis and help him in fighting this disease, Mom. I don't mind that I am in a wheelchair. I'm sad that other kids have to sit in them. They're not as happy as I am. I would like to meet him."

Mom said, "One day, you will."

In July, an eight-member film crew traveled to Salt Lake City to videotape a profile. I had been selected as one of the five national finalists for this first-time award. I didn't believe I had the slightest chance of winning the award since the other candidates had outstanding achievements and were better known by MDA's national office in Tucson, Arizona.

I decided that I would tell my story — faith and family. The director of the film crew said he never met anyone who spoke as if they were reading from a teleprompter. I told him, "I know my lines because I've been reading the same script and playing the same role ever since Dad bought that magazine in 1960." Not coincidently, I was notified on August 13, 1992 that I had won — Dad's seventieth birthday!

Before Labor Day I went to Los Angeles to do a taped interview with Sally Jessy Raphael for the Telethon. Her subject was the Americans with Disabilities Act. After the interview, Sally said, "Steve, you've got a great mouth. There are a lot of people in this business who wish they had a mouth like yours."

I knew that she wasn't referring to my crooked smile, which is symptomatic of my disease. I was grateful for Sally's compliment.

When I got to Las Vegas, it was thrilling to meet Jerry Lewis. I told him how much his volunteerism and humanitarianism had always touched me. He has raised over one billion dollars for research and services to literally tens of thousands of us with these diseases.

I was informed that the telethon's co-host, Leeza Gibbons, would present me with the award in the final hours of the show.

I learned that Leeza was the honorary chair of the Spinal Muscular Atrophy division of MDA. I wondered whether she had ever known someone with my disease. Was she genuinely interested in my disease or was her involvement superficial? What was motivating her to sacrifice two days of her life, stay awake for over 24 hours, and talk about a disease that she didn't have?

Naturally, this was not the first time that I had heard the name Leeza Gibbons. I had watched her for years on Entertainment Tonight, television's daily entertainment magazine. Through watching the show my knowledge of Leeza was limited to this — that she was more beautiful than Mary Hart and was blessed with a better pair of legs. I also vaguely remembered that she was once linked to 80's pop icon, Billy Idol.

I must confess that accompanying me to Las Vegas were certain assumptions, myths and stereotypes about this woman. The cynical side of me told me that she was probably one in a parade of other former beauty queens who was capitalizing on her looks and ability to read a teleprompter.

I knew that I would meet her as a result of her telethon duties, but wasn't particularly looking forward to that meeting. Well, I did want to see those legs up close and personal, but that was it. I dreaded the polite, chilly reception that I assumed would greet me. After all, she was a star, a celebrity, and one of the most glamorous women on television. What did we have in common? What would we talk about?

I anticipated that we would exchange the normal pleasantries that prevail at such occasions. I fully expected that she would introduce herself, thank me for coming to the Telethon, and congratulate me for receiving the award. That would be all. She would pretend that she was needed elsewhere and swiftly move on. I imagined that would be the extent of my moment with Leeza Gibbons,

There was a twist to the annual fundraising rituals. MDA had appointed 15 adults with neuromuscular diseases to its National Task Force on Public Awareness to emphasize MDA's support on the recently enacted civil rights law known as The Americans with Disabilities Act. With 15 wheelchairs crammed into the backstage green room prior to our on-air introduction I felt a little like a showgirl, without the sequins of course. Amidst the whirlwind of floor directors, makeup artists, and telethon groupies, I first saw her. She was talking to a member of the task force. When our eyes met she immediately flashed her radiant smile and approached me.

I was surprised that she already knew my name and had viewed the videotape that MDA had prepared to coincide with my appearance. What impressed me the most about Leeza on that first meeting was how comfortable she was and how accepted she made me feel. She wasn't aloof or patronizing. Her body language reassured me of that because she crouched down in order to converse with me at my level, rather than require me to bend my neck backwards and shout over the din of the room.

The next thing that struck me was her intensity of focus. Her attention never wandered. It was as if no one else was in that room. She made me feel unique and special. She wanted to know about my upbringing, about the magazine that my Father gave me when I was four years old, as well as my feelings about discrimination against people with disabilities.

These were not typical cocktail inquiries. They penetrated to the depths of who I was as a person. The answers to such questions defined who I was and the fact that she had asked them with such genuine interest both honored and humbled me. She promised that we would talk more the next day when she presented me with the Personal Achievement Award. The skeptic inside of me told me that she was too good to be true. But something else was telling me that Leeza

The Third Opinion

had a goodness and compassion worth trusting.

The following day before the show closed with Jerry Lewis singing his rendition of "You'll Never Walk Alone," Leeza introduced my vignette as I was positioned on the stage between Jerry Lewis and her. As the video closed, Jerry Lewis was standing on my left side and Leeza was down at my level again to the right of my wheelchair. I was astonished when, before she put the microphone in front of me, she said, "Your Mommy is proud of you!"

Until that point the weekend had been somewhat bittersweet. I was sad that my mother wasn't there. I felt that it was as much her award as it was mine. I could not have reached that point in my life without the consistent support of my father, mother, brother Bill, and sisters, Carole and Judy. Now, with Leeza uttering those words of reassurance I knew that somewhere and somehow my mother was there. I explained to Leeza as she accompanied me off stage how much if meant to me that she had acknowledged my mother so candidly with not only me, but also millions of viewers. I expressed my desire to keep in touch and she reciprocated.

That evening as I sat on a plane going back to Salt Lake City, I held my award on my lap. Yet, on my mind, were the moments, those few precious moments I had spent with Leeza.

Chapter 30

Six months after I met Leeza Gibbons, I visited a man whose love and admiration for FDR are as strong as mine. We were the only two people in the room, besides a secret service agent. I was doing a media tour across the country. He was running for President.

Bill Clinton was only two weeks away from his election night victory when we met on the outskirts of Detroit during a campaign stop. He was sipping tea for his then chronicallyhoarse throat. His advance people said he only had five minutes. We chatted for half an hour.

We discussed our mutual respect for FDR, our childhood challenges and the need for universal health care coverage for Americans with disabilities. I explained to him that for the promise of the ADA to fully become a reality, two remaining issues required national attention — health insurance and personal attendant care services. I pointed out that for many persons with disabilities, working was a disincentive, if it meant losing their Medicaid card. I also recommended that, if elected, Mr. Clinton should incorporate attendant care services into his National Youth Corps idea that would enable college students to pay off their government loans by working for individuals with disabilities.

He listened intently. His eyes were totally focused on me for the entirety of the meeting. His questions were sincere and substantive. I was amazed by his capacity to concentrate solely on our discussion.

He didn't seem preoccupied or frenzied, even though he was in the final stages of the campaign. What I'll never forget about my half hour with Bill Clinton was his genuine warmth and tenderness.

Unlike many other public officials whom I've met or counseled,

Mr. Clinton was not awkward around me. In fact, we sat as close to each other as possible, even though we had the entire room to ourselves. It was as if we were old law school pals. That's how approachable and unassuming he was.

At the close of our meeting, I said, "Governor, if you are elected President of the United States, in a couple of weeks, you have the commitment to do more things to help Americans with disabilities than any other president before you. I know that you care about this segment of our society. I can see it in your eyes. I can hear it in your voice and I can feel it in your soul. It has been a great honor meeting you."

Mr. Clinton delicately clasped both of my hands within his large right hand and held them for more than a minute. He said, "Thank you. I have really appreciated our visit. Thank you."

It is so obvious how a man with such charisma and warmth gained national political prominence in such a short time. Bill Clinton has the gift of leaving a lasting, positive impression out of a momentary contact.

Much to my delight in January, 1993, I was contacted by Burt Dubrow, Sally Jessy Raphael's executive producer, saying that Sally was interested in doing a show about me. Dubrow said that I would need to pitch a concept that would be provocative enough and exciting enough to be "show-worthy." I told Burt that I believed that we could feature other individuals with disabilities who were experiencing problems coping with their limitations and I could encourage them to accept the reality of who they were and what they were capable of achieving in their lives.

On the day of the show, Dubrow kept saying, "Don't blow this Mikita." He said he was joking, but I knew he was skeptical about my ability to pull it off.

The show opened with a young couple whose two-year-old son, Max, had cerebral palsy. Kim, the mother, was extremely bitter and angry that her son was so disabled and would never do the things that other children could do. She was inconsolable. I was astonished at the depth of her bitterness two years after Max's birth.

I told Max's parents they had a beautiful son whose spirit and innocence really touched me. I recommended they focus on Max's beauty, his life and his love and to stop comparing him with every other child. It was time to let go of their anger and rage. It was time to begin living, embracing and accepting their son, not wishing and hoping that he was someone else.

Their time for grieving had ended. It was time to take one day at a time and to be grateful for that day and that child. Feeling sorry for themselves would not help him or them. Loving him would.

The next segment of the show involved an overprotective mother whose teenage son, Rob, flatly refused to comply with either his doctor's orders or his mother's wishes. Rob had a deteriorating muscle disorder that was affecting his leg strength. To slow the atrophy, his doctor prescribed splints for his knees, ankles and feet.

Rob ignored his mother's repeated pleas to wear his splints. His excuse was that his friends with whom he went rollerblading ridiculed him for wearing them.

I told the mother that she needed to stop badgering Rob. It was his life, his legs and his health. If he didn't want to wear the splints, nothing that she did or said at this point would help him see the wisdom of her or the doctor's advice. Obviously, peer acceptance was more important to him than his muscles.

I turned to Rob and reminded him that if his friends were truly friends, they would not mock him for having to wear the leg splints. I also told him that he really wouldn't be losing his identity, if he were to give up rollerblading. I told Rob that he was an extremely handsome and likeable guy, and that if I looked like him, I wouldn't be a bachelor.

The last segment featured a mother and father complaining that their 21-year-old quadriplegic son, Michael, was wasting his life away in his bedroom. They said that Michael had given up on everything and everyone, including himself. Michael was shutting the world out. He was even afraid to spend time with his lovely four-year-old daughter.

I told Michael that there was too much life left for him to live, to just vegetate. Appealing to his memory of his high school football career, I explained to him that he had been on the sidelines long enough. I challenged Michael to get back into the game of life — to be a player again, not an uninterested spectator.

I explained to Michael that this new game would demand the same degree of commitment and effort that being a football player required. I told him there was so much more for him left to do than spend the day in his bedroom. His little girl needed him. That was a wonderful start. She was enough incentive for him to begin anew.

By the end of the show, it seemed like we had just spent an hour in Sally's living room, not a television studio. Burt Dubrow was jubilant. It was a great show.

I received hundreds of well wishes from around the country, including at least twenty marriage proposals! At one point of the show, I joked to Sally that I was single and "entertaining applications" from worthy candidates. Apparently, some viewers did not find any humor with the remark and took me seriously to the extent that they sent photographs and resumes detailing their matrimonial eligibility.

Particularly gratifying were the calls and letters from parents of children with disabilities who thanked me for my advice and perspective. They thanked me for giving them the courage to continue the day-to-day battle of hope, faith and perseverance that many of us wage. They didn't feel so alone.

Before the beginning of the show, Sally took me aside and said, "This show reaches millions of people every day. You don't know whose life you will touch, but you will touch someone. I promise you. It's like throwing a pebble in a pond. That one pebble will cause waves to reach the shore."

My pebble, fortunately, reached many shorelines even in such far off places as Australia and Zimbabwe! Every person who called or wrote a letter stated that they wanted more. They asked whether I had written a book or produced any videos. This book is another pebble from me.

Besides writing this book, practicing law and teaching at the Brigham Young University and University of Utah law schools, I continue to share my message with audiences across the country.

When I completed this book five years ago I had two goals. One was to celebrate my fortieth birthday with family and friends; the other was to attend the dedication of the FDR Memorial in Washington, D.C. The birthday was a memorable evening spent at my favorite Salt Lake City restaurant. But the trip to Washington did not occur until March 2000, when I was invited to testify before Congress regarding increased funding for spinal muscular atrophy research. Before delivering my remarks I took time to pay homage to the man who gave me my dream four decades ago.

As I told the congressional subcommittee, I have been living the dream of FDR inside the nightmare of SMA. I never conceived that I would be discussing a possible cure during my lifetime. The word "cure" had never been part of my equation or the third opinion. And for all intents and purposes, it still isn't. My dream and prayer for a cure are not for my life, but for the tragically shortened lives of my young friends who are ruthlessly stalked by this serial killer, as well as for the unborn children whose bodies and minds could be spared the buffetings of this disease.

But my quest for a cure is not a solitary one. My life has been blessed with my best friend, Leeza Gibbons. As the world sees it, how we became friends probably makes little sense. But we had courage enough to take a risk and step outside our comfort zones long enough to listen, to love, and to make a difference in each other's lives. We discarded the stereotypes surrounding "celebrity" and "disability," and received the priceless gift of our moments spent together. Although Leeza has never seen the magazine piece on FDR that inspired me, no one understands more perfectly the meaning of the third opinion. It is about loving ourselves and each other enough to stop and realize that each one of us has purpose, meaning, and beauty in our lives: that each of us matters.

The third opinion defined a four year old's dream and it continues to propel a special friendship and strengthen an extraordinary bond.